MW00851933

CAMPAIGN 410

EAST AFRICA CAMPAIGN 1940–41

The Battle for the Horn of Africa

PIER PAOLO BATTISTELLI

ILLUSTRATED BY JOHNNY SHUMATE

OSPREY PUBLISHING
Bloomsbury Publishing Plc
Kemp House, Chawley Park, Cumnor Hill, Oxford OX2 9PH, UK
29 Earlsfort Terrace, Dublin 2, Ireland
1385 Broadway, 5th Floor, New York, NY 10018, USA
E-mail: info@ospreypublishing.com
www.ospreypublishing.com

OSPREY is a trademark of Osprey Publishing Ltd

First published in Great Britain in 2024

© Osprey Publishing Ltd, 2024

All rights reserved. No part of this publication may be reproduced or
transmitted in any form or by any means, electronic or mechanical,
including photocopying, recording, or any information storage or retrieval
system, without prior permission in writing from the publishers.

A catalogue record for this book is available from the British Library.

ISBN: PB 9781472860712; eBook 9781472860705;
ePDF 9781472860699; XML 9781472860729

24 25 26 27 28   10 9 8 7 6 5 4 3 2 1

Maps by Bounford.com
3D BEVs by Paul Kime
Index by Alison Worthington
Typeset by PDQ Digital Media Solutions, Bungay, UK
Printed by Repro India Ltd.

MIX
Paper
FSC   FSC® C047271

Osprey Publishing supports the Woodland Trust, the UK's leading woodland
conservation charity.

To find out more about our authors and books visit
www.ospreypublishing.com. Here you will find extracts, author
interviews, details of forthcoming events and the option to sign up for
our newsletter.

Acknowledgements

The author gratefully acknowledges the help and support provided by
Nikolai Bogdanovic, Professor Richard Carrier, Piero Crociani, Dr Christopher
Pugsley, Dr Klaus Schmider (Sandhurst) and the series editor, Brianne Bellio.

Dedication

To Nikolai, remembering the good work together.

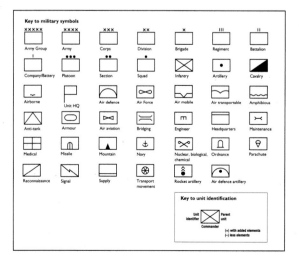

Front cover main illustration: The assault at Keren, 16 March 1941.
(Johnny Shumate)
Title page image: British victory parade after the capture of Asmara.
(Photo by Bettmann/Getty Images)

CONTENTS

ORIGINS OF THE CAMPAIGN

As Italy entered World War II on 10 June 1940, British positions in the Mediterranean, Middle East and East Africa were seriously endangered. Italy could rely upon superior forces, thanks to the French surrender and also to the fact that Britain's first and foremost concern, and allocation of manpower, was the defence of the homeland from the threat of a German invasion. For Britain's colonies in Africa, the main threat was from the Italian colonies in Libya and East Africa, where, from 1935–36, Italy had seized the last independent African country, Ethiopia, moving from its colonies of Eritrea and Italian Somaliland. Italian East Africa, Mussolini's much-boasted new 'Roman Empire', now represented a significant threat. Potentially, the Italians could move from Libya into Egypt, reaching the strategically vital Suez Canal and the Nile, which could be used to link its two colonies with attacks from the north and the south. By doing so, Italian East Africa would be relieved from isolation, enabling the Italians to threaten Britain's important regional colonies and mandates. While an invasion of the Middle East could be launched, the Italians could also use the Red Sea to access the Indian Ocean, threatening communications with India, if not the colony itself. On paper, this was a potential war-winning scenario.

The fact that Italy had no actual plans to drive the British forces out of Egypt or to link up Libya with East Africa did not diminish the potential danger, and, in September 1940, the British positions in Kenya and Sudan were reinforced to deal with the situation. The relative Italian inactivity since the summer of 1940, when their forces attacked and seized British Somaliland along with some frontier outposts in Libya, Sudan and Kenya, enabled the British Commander-in-Chief in the Middle East, General Archibald Wavell, to develop a main strategy, simultaneously enforcing it in the various theatres of war. The British offensive started in December 1940 in Egypt, soon leading to the invasion of eastern Libya (Cyrenaica) and the Italian defeat at Beda Fomm in February 1941, a prelude to the pincer offensive that was started against Italian East Africa from the south and the north. Both had promising, albeit not very dramatic, results. The situation became more complicated between February and March 1941, when German troops arrived in North Africa and Wavell had to send an expeditionary force to Greece in order to help the country face an imminent German onslaught.

By April 1941, British positions in Africa and the Mediterranean again faced a serious threat, this time a more tangible one. General Rommel's

Mussolini parading down Via dell'Impero (Empire Street) in Rome. His idea of a new Roman Empire clashed with reality and collapsed soon after Italy's entry into the war. (Photo by Keystone-France/Gamma-Rapho via Getty Images)

offensive in Libya and the German invasion of the Balkans, coupled with the start of the Iraqi insurgency, saw British forces seriously outnumbered and overstretched, with the East Africa campaign providing the only solution to the crisis. Thanks to the victory at Keren and the swift advance from Kenya, Italian forces were pushed away from the sea and completely isolated. This made it possible to achieve a swift victory, which came in May with the Italian surrender at Amba Alagi, enabling Wavell to start redeploying his forces to deal with the situation in North Africa and the Middle East. Even though Wavell had to face the loss of the Balkans and Crete, he was able to halt Rommel's advance, mostly due to the positions held at Tobruk, while dealing with the insurgency in Iraq and, later on, with the Vichy French colony of Syria. When Germany invaded the Soviet Union in June 1941, the threat against the British had mostly been neutralized due to the successes achieved in East Africa, where Emperor Haile Selassie had been restored to power.

By September 1941, the East Africa campaign had reached its turning point, resulting in a complete British victory, achieved due to the efforts of troops – especially Indian and South, West and East African troops – which performed extraordinarily, helping to overturn the strategic balance in the entire region. In September, all that was left was a series of mopping-up operations of the remaining Italian garrisons, which fought valiantly, albeit without hope, to the last. The fall of Gondar in November 1941 marked the official end to a campaign that, even though underrated and all too often ignored, played a decisive role in the history of World War II.

CHRONOLOGY

1940

10 June	Italy declares war on France and Great Britain.
25 June	French surrender. French Somaliland is taken over by Vichy France, disrupting the British defence plan for Somaliland.
1 July	Arrival in Kenya of 1st South African and 23rd Nigerian Brigades.
4 July	Italian seizure of Kassala and Gallabat.
5–18 August	Italian attack on British Somaliland; evacuation of British troops from Berbera.
8–18 September	Arrival in Sudan of 5th Indian Division.
2 October	Arrival in Kenya of 2nd and 5th South African Brigades; formation of 1st South African Division and 11th and 12th African Divisions.
28 October	Italy attacks Greece.
1 November	General Cunningham assumes command of British forces in East Africa from Lieutenant-General Dickinson.
6 November	5th Indian Division attacks Gallabat and Metemma.
2 December	General Wavell's conference with Generals Platt and Cunningham on offensive operations against Italian East Africa.
9 December	Start of the Operation *Compass* offensive in North Africa.

1941

7 January	Arrival in Sudan of 4th Indian Division.
15–18 January	Advance of 11th and 12th African Divisions in Italian Somaliland; capture of El Yibo and Mega.
19 January	Opening of offensive campaign against Italian East Africa, seizure of Kassala and advance of 4th Indian Division towards Sabderat and 5th Indian Division towards Aicota.
20 January	Emperor Haile Selassie arrives at Abyssinian border.
28 January	First combat with Italian troops at Barentu.
1 February	Barentu and Agordat are captured.
4 February	First advance into Keren defences and Italian counter-attack.
7 February	East African troops enter Italian Somaliland. Italian troops are defeated in Libya at Beda Fomm.

11–14 February	Capture of Afmadu and Kismayu by 11th African Division.
12 February	First assault on Keren defences.
19 February	Crossing of the Juba River and Italian withdrawal from Somaliland.
25 February	12th African Division captures Mogadishu.
4 March	Gideon Force captures Dembacha.
15 March	Second assault on Keren defences.
16 March	Landing at and capture of Berbera; British Somaliland is back in British hands.
21 March	12th African Division seizes Neghelli and concludes its advance into Ethiopia.
25–29 March	11th African Division advances into Ethiopia, seizing Harar and Diredawa.
27 March	Keren falls; Italian forces withdraw inland.
1 April	Asmara is captured.
3 April	Capture of Debra Markos.
6 April	Addis Ababa surrenders, bringing to an end the first phase of the campaign; 4th Indian Division is transferred to Egypt.
8 April	Capture of Massawa.
26 April	Capture of Dessie.
5 May	Emperor Haile Selassie enters Addis Ababa.
10–17 May	Battle of the Lakes.
19 May	Capture of Amba Alagi and surrender of Amedeo d'Aosta.
23 May	Some 8,000 Italian troops led by Colonel Maraventano surrender at Agibar.
6 July	General Gazzera, who succeeded Amedeo d'Aosta in command, surrenders at Gambela.
27 September	Attack at Wolchefit paves the way for the advance to Gondar.
21 November	Capture of Kulkaber.
27 November	Capture of Gondar and end of organized Italian resistance in East Africa.

OPPOSING COMMANDERS

BRITISH

The East Africa campaign was the proving ground for a good number of British and South African commanders, who in many cases would later prove themselves fighting on other fronts. **General Sir William Platt**, commander of the forces in Sudan, was born in Cheshire in 1885 and commissioned in the Northumberland Fusiliers in 1905, serving then in India. During World War I, Platt served on the Western Front, where he was wounded four times and mentioned in despatches (MiD). Promoted to captain in November 1914 and major in December 1916, Platt later served as a general staff officer in 21st Division and, from 1917, the II Australian and New Zealand Army Corps (subsequently re-designated British XXII Army Corps). Temporarily appointed lieutenant-colonel in 1918, Platt attended the Staff College at Camberley in 1919 and 1920, married in 1921 and served in Ireland until 1922. After two years in Egypt, Platt served in 1927 as Deputy Assistant Adjutant General in the Adjutant General Staff at the War Office. After a tour of duty in command

Major-General William Platt inspecting troops in the Middle East along with his superior commander, General Sir Archibald Wavell. (Photo by Popperfoto via Getty Images)

General Alfred Reade Godwin-Austen, pictured along with General Thomas Riddell-Webster in London in early 1944. At the time, the two were Vice-Quartermaster General and Quartermaster General to the Forces. (Photo by Popperfoto via Getty Images)

of the 2nd Wiltshire Regiment, Platt was promoted to colonel in 1933 and appointed first staff officer with 3rd Division. From 1934, he commanded 7th Infantry Brigade, then Platt was made aide-de-camp to the king in 1938 and promoted to major-general, taking over command of the Sudan Defence Force, referred to in Arabic as the 'Kaid', or leader of the army. In January 1941, Platt was promoted to lieutenant-general and took command of the northern pincer of the two-pronged offensive against Italian East Africa. Well esteemed by other commanders, who remarked on the grip he had on the situation, Platt is considered the victor of the battle of Keren and, along with Cunningham, the victor of the entire campaign. This earned him a knighthood, promotion to general in 1943 and, between 1941 and 1945, being made General Officer Commanding (GOC) of East Africa Command. Along with raising African troops for the campaign in Burma, he also led the campaign that ended with the seizure of the Vichy France-occupied Madagascar in 1942. After retiring from active duty in 1945, Platt, an honorary colonel commandant of the Wiltshire Regiment until 1954, lived in the Lake District, taking an interest in art. He died in 1975, aged 90.

General Sir Alfred Reade Godwin-Austen, Platt's first subordinate commander, was born in Surrey in 1889 to a family with an outstanding military tradition. Commissioned in 1909 in the South Wales Borderers, he fought during World War I in the Middle East, distinguishing himself at Gallipoli and in Palestine and Mesopotamia, winning the Military Cross (MC). After serving as a general staff officer with 13th Division during the war, between 1924 and 1925, Godwin-Austen attended the Staff College at Camberley, later serving in various appointments at the War Office until he was made instructor at the Royal Military College Sandhurst. Commander of the 2nd Duke of Cornwall's Light Infantry from 1936–37, he then served with the Military Mission to the Egyptian Army until 1938, before taking command of 14th Infantry Brigade in Palestine. In 1939, Godwin-Austen was promoted to major-general and was given command of 8th Infantry Division in Palestine, which was disbanded in February 1940. Godwin-Austen was then given command of 2nd (African) Division being formed in Kenya, but before he could take over he was sent to British Somaliland to command the British forces facing the Italian invasion. Albeit largely outnumbered, Godwin-Austen successfully faced the onslaught and withdrew his forces to Aden, having suffered the loss of just 260 men. This led Winston Churchill to believe that Somaliland had been abandoned without fighting, and he asked for Godwin-Austen to be suspended from duty and be put under inquiry. Wavell successfully objected to the request and had Godwin-Austen take over command of 2nd, later 12th, (African) Division, which he successfully led during the East African campaign, seizing Italian Somaliland and entering Addis Ababa on 6 April 1941. In September 1941, General Claude Auchinleck, the new Commander-in-Chief in the Middle East, appointed Godwin-Austen commander of the newly formed XIII Army Corps (formed within 8th Army from the Western Desert Force). Soon, Godwin-Austen clashed with his superior commanders on the proper strategy to adopt facing Rommel's February 1942 offensive into Western Cyrenaica. Godwin-Austen eventually asked to be relieved from command, partly because of Churchill's continued hostile attitude. Godwin-Austen later served in the Directorate of Tactical Research at the War Office and was assistant to the commander of the Staff College, Camberley. Eventually appointed Vice-Quartermaster General in 1943, in 1945 he was appointed Quartermaster General in India, being promoted to general and granted a knighthood. He retired from active duty in 1947, living as a bachelor and a keen tennis player until he had to stop due to illness that led to his death in 1963 at the age of 73.

Lieutenant-General Sir Noel Monson de la Poer Beresford-Peirse, the son of an Indian Army colonel, was born in 1887 in Ireland. After being commissioned in 1907 in the Royal Artillery, he served in Egypt, Mesopotamia and France during World War I. Mentioned in despatches and awarded a Distinguished Service Order (DSO), after the war he attended the Staff College at Camberley and was later posted to India. After serving as an instructor at the Senior Officers' School at Belgaum in India and being made aide-de-camp to the king, in 1938 (after commanding the divisional artillery) he took command of 4th Indian Division, with which he went to Egypt. In December 1940, Beresford-Peirse's division spearheaded the attack against the Italian positions at Sidi Barrani in Egypt, the first step of the successful Operation *Compass*. 4th Indian Division was withdrawn from Egypt in December 1940 and transferred to Sudan, where it took part in operations in Italian East Africa. Beresford-Peirse's successful leadership and command displayed at Keren earned him, in March 1941, promotion to lieutenant-general, a knighthood and, in April that year, command of the Western Desert Force (later XIII Army Corps) in Egypt. After the failure of the short-lived offensive against Sollum in June (Operation *Battleaxe*), Beresford-Peirse was sent back to Sudan, where he was made GOC of British forces. In April 1942, Beresford-Peirse was posted back to India, where he took command of XV Corps and, from June, became General Officer Commander-in-Chief of Southern Command India. Appointed Welfare General of India Command between 1945 and 1947, Beresford-Peirse retired from active duty in 1947, living near Salisbury, where he died aged 65 in 1953.

Fighting alongside Beresford-Peirse's 4th Indian Division was **Lieutenant-General Sir Lewis Macclesfield Heath's** 5th Indian Division, which earned its own distinction. Heath was born in 1885 in India, the son of a civil servant. After attending the Royal Military Academy at Sandhurst, he joined the Indian Army in 1905, being transferred the next year to the 11th Sikh Regiment. During World War I, he served as an artilleryman in Egypt and Mesopotamia, receiving a MiD and winning an MC. He was also badly injured, suffering the loss of an eye and permanent damage to his left arm. After the war, from 1919–22, Heath served in Afghanistan and East Persia, before being appointed instructor at the Senior Officers' School at Belgaum and taking over command of the Wana Brigade in 1936. In 1939, as World War II broke out, Heath was in command of the Deccan District before being promoted to major-general and being given command of the newly formed 5th Indian Division. After the victory at Keren, Heath returned to India, where, after being promoted to lieutenant-general, he commanded III Indian Army Corps in the defence of northern Malaya. Taken prisoner at Singapore, he retired from active duty soon after being released from captivity in 1945. He died in Bath in 1954, aged 68.

Commander of 7th Indian Infantry Brigade, **Lieutenant-General Sir Harold Rawdon Briggs** successfully led the Briggs' Force against Eritrea. Born in 1894 in Minnesota in the United States, Briggs attended Sandhurst Military Academy before joining the Indian Army in 1914. He served during World War I in Mesopotamia and Palestine with 4th King's (Liverpool) Regiment, and later in 31st Punjab Regiment. After attending the Staff College at Quetta and taking part in the Waziristan campaign, Briggs was given command of the 2nd Baluch Regiment in 1937. Promoted to brigadier in 1940, he was given command of 7th Indian Brigade in Eritrea, which he used to form the Briggs' Force, acting independently from the rest of the division. Serving with 4th Indian Division in North Africa, Briggs successfully faced Rommel's April 1941 offensive into Cyrenaica, earning a DSO and promotion to major-general in early 1942. Given command of 5th Indian Division, he fought in the May–June 1942 Gazala battle,

Major-General Heath and Air Commodore Slatter illustrate to South African and Rhodesian Air Force crews the area of the battle for Keren. (Photo by Mirrorpix/Mirrorpix via Getty Images)

General Sir Alan Cunningham, photographed in 1945, when he was High Commissioner of Palestine. (Photo by Popperfoto via Getty Images)

after which the division was sent to Iraq and then to India. In 1944 and 1945, Briggs successfully led the division in the Arakan campaign, relieving the besieged garrison of Kohima, much to the praise of 14th Army commander General Slim. Promoted to lieutenant-general, Briggs briefly served as General Officer Commander-in-Chief of Eastern Command, India, before being appointed General Officer Commander-in-Chief, Burma, until 1948. Retired in that year, Briggs served as Director of Operations during the Malaya counter-insurgency. He died in Cyprus in 1952 at the age of 58.

The southern pincer moving against the Italians in East Africa was led by the British commander in Kenya, **General Sir Alan Gordon Cunningham**. Born in 1887 in Dublin, Cunningham (whose older brother was Admiral A. B. Cunningham, First Sea Lord from 1943) was commissioned in the Royal Artillery in 1906 and served during World War I with the Royal Horse Artillery in France, receiving five MiDs and being awarded both an MC and a DSO. Graduating from the Naval Staff College in 1925, Cunningham also attended the Imperial Defence College in 1937 before being given, unusually for a naval graduate, command of the artillery of 1st Division. In 1938, he was promoted to major-general and given command of 5th Anti-Aircraft Division, the first of a series of commands with the home forces that preceded his transfer to Kenya in October 1940, where he took over command of British forces. The campaign leading to the seizure of Italian Somaliland saw Cunningham at his best, his troops moving extraordinarily fast and their supplies being provided all through their advance. This led to him receiving the Knight Commander of the Order of the Bath and, in August 1941, the command of 8th Army in North Africa, which he led during the November 1941 Operation *Crusader*. Even though this offensive

Major-General George Edwin Brink (fourth from the left) inspecting a Marmon-Herrington Mk I armoured car from the 1st South African Division in Kenya in October 1940. (Photo by Keystone/Hulton Archive/Getty Images)

was successful, Cunningham showed a lack of energy and fell into a depressed state, which led to his removal from command, hospitalization under an assumed name and a transfer back home. Between 1942 and 1945, Cunningham held several command positions in Britain, including those of commandant of the Staff College at Camberley, GOC of the Northern Ireland District and General Officer Commander-in-Chief of Eastern Command. Promoted to general in 1945, he served as High Commissioner and Commander-in-Chief in Palestine until his retirement 1948, when he was awarded the Knight Grand Cross of the Order of St Michael and St George. Colonel Commandant of the Royal Artillery from 1948–54, Cunningham lived as a keen fisherman in Kent until his death, at the age of 95, in 1983.

Lieutenant-General George Edwin Brink, born in 1889 in the Orange Free State in South Africa, was Cunningham's first subordinate commander. After various civilian roles, Brink joined the Union Defence Forces in 1913, being commissioned in the following year. During World War I, he served in the South West Africa Campaign before being promoted to major and becoming a staff officer in 1916, when he served in German East Africa. After attending the Imperial Staff College in 1919, Brink entered the staff of the South African Military College, which he commanded briefly in 1933 before being appointed commander of the Western Cape Command. Director of Army Training until 1938, Brink was made Deputy Chief of General Staff in June of that year. In October 1940, Brink was given command of 1st South African Division, which he led successfully in East Africa and then in North Africa following its redeployment. In March 1942, Brink relinquished command to Dan Pienaar following an accident that had him declared unfit for field duty. Thereafter, Brink commanded the Inland Area Command and was in charge of the South African forces' demobilization. Retired from active duty in 1946, he was promoted to lieutenant-general in the reserve. He died in 1971 in Natal, aged 81.

Lieutenant-General Sir Harry Edward de Robillard Wetherall, born in 1889 in London to a military family, was commissioned in 1909 and served in France during World War I with the Gloucestershire Regiment, earning an MC and a DSO. Promoted to major in 1927, Wetherall was chief staff officer for weapons training in Scottish Command between 1930 and 1936, when he was given command of the 1st York and Lancaster Regiment in Palestine. In 1938, he was given command of the 19th Infantry Brigade. In 1941, Wetherall took over command of 11th (African) Infantry Division, which he successfully led during the East African campaign before his appointment as GOC in East Africa. This was followed by an

Major-General Arthur Reginald Chater and his wife, Diana. (King's College London: Liddell Hart Centre for Military Archives, Chater 10/8)

appointment as GOC in Ceylon in 1943, a position he held until 1945. Knighted, Wetherall retired in 1946 to Somerset, where he died aged 90 in 1979.

Two commanders deserve a special mention. The first is **Major-General Arthur Reginald Chater**, a Royal Marine officer born in 1896 and commissioned in 1913. During World War I, he fought at Antwerp, Gallipoli and Zeebrugge, serving after the war with the Egyptian Army, which gave him command of the Sudan Camel Corps. Made governor of Sudan in 1941, Chater evacuated to Aden in the wake of the Italian offensive, only to return less than a year later in command of the British Somaliland Forces. In 1943, he was made commander of the Royal Marines Portsmouth Division before being appointed Director of Combined Operations for India and South-East Asia in 1944. Retired in 1948, Chater died aged 82 in 1979.

Major-General Orde Charles Wingate, born in 1903 in India to a military family, was commissioned in the Royal Artillery in 1926, soon enrolling himself in an Arabic language course at the School of Oriental Studies. In spite of some non-military traits of his personality, Wingate enjoyed a successful career thanks to his buoyant and unconventional attitude. Attached to the Sudan Defence Force in 1928, Wingate travelled extensively in Africa and, after serving at home and unsuccessfully trying to join the Staff College, Camberley, he was posted to Palestine as an intelligence officer with 5th Division. Repatriated, he pulled some strings to be posted to Khartoum, where he organized the Abyssinian Patriots (called Arbegnouc, or Arbegnoch in English), starting a guerrilla war against the Italians and soon being joined by Emperor Haile Selassie. In spite of his skills and successes, chief among them the restoration of the emperor to his throne, Wingate suffered from depression and attempted suicide. Thanks to Wingate's influence and to Winston Churchill's attention, and despite adverse reports from his superiors, Wingate managed to be posted to India in March 1942. There, promoted to colonel, he was given command of 77th Indian Infantry Brigade, which he used to create the Long Range Penetration Units, known as Chindits. His unconventional methods were criticized, and it has to be noted that

Orde Wingate entering Addis Ababa on horseback in the wake of Emperor Haile Selassie. (IDF Archive, public domain, via Wikimedia Commons)

the Chindit force was crippled when it operated behind the Japanese lines in Burma. Although the actual role and impact of this force is still debated, Wingate nevertheless became a name in the wake of T. E. Lawrence and other British officers who created the first unconventional methods of warfare. Promoted to acting major-general in September 1943, Wingate launched Operation *Thursday* in March 1944, a larger-scale penetration behind the Japanese lines, and died on the 24th of that same month in an aircraft accident at the age of 41.

ITALIAN

General of the Air Force (Generale d'Armata Aerea) Amedeo di Savoia, Duke of Aosta (Duca di Aosta), was born in Turin in 1898, a member of the Savoia-Aosta branch of the Italian royal family. Educated at St David's College in England, he joined the Italian Army as a volunteer aged 16 in 1915, soon earning promotion in the field to lieutenant and, at the end of World War I, to captain. After the war, he joined his uncle in a geographical expedition in Somaliland, before returning home in 1920 to get his Italian high school degree. According to an apocryphal story, the following year he went to Belgian Congo, having been sent away after cracking a joke at the expense of the King of Italy. Returning to Italy in 1923, he joined the army again, being promoted to major. He then attended university, graduating in law, which, in 1924 Italy, was considered the equivalent of a philosophy degree. In 1926, after obtaining a pilot brevet, Amedeo returned to Africa for a few years before being given command of an artillery regiment in 1931. In 1932, Amedeo joined the Italian Air Force (Regia Aeronautica), soon being given command of a reconnaissance wing and then a fighter wing. Promoted to brigadier in 1934, he was then promoted two years later to major-general and, later that same year, lieutenant-general. In 1939, he was made Governor General of Italian East Africa (*Africa Orientale Italiana*) and Viceroy of Ethiopia. Isolated at Amba Alagi, facing the British attack on 14 May 1941, Amedeo asked Mussolini for permission to surrender, which he did five days later. It is well known that he received 'the honour of the arms', which is when the surrendering commander passes in parade the victorious forces as if he were the victor, which became the most known feature of the Italian forces during the entire campaign. Sent to Kenya, Amedeo became ill from tuberculosis and malaria and died on 3 March 1942, aged 43. Lacking personal records, most of Amedeo di Savoia's biography is based on second- or third-hand sources, which clearly attempt to portray him as a gallant and valorous soldier and an adventurer. The truth, which can be easily ascertained from the available records of his conduct of the campaign in East Africa in 1940–41, shows a commander lacking the necessary professional skills and experience, unimaginative and strongly tied to the directives sent to him by Mussolini and his Chief of General Staff, Field Marshal Pietro Badoglio. There can be

Generale d'Armata Aerea Amedeo di Savoia duca di Aosta, photographed in Ethiopia during the early stages of the campaign. (From *L'Illustrazione Italiana*, Year LXVIII, No 19, 11 May 1941/ De Agostini Picture Library/ Contributor/via Getty Images)

General Claudio Trezzani, seen here in a post-war photograph, was to all intents Amedeo d'Aosta's deputy and the actual brains behind the Italian strategy in East Africa. (Italian Ministry of Defence, public domain, via Wikimedia Commons)

General Luigi Frusci, the Italian commander defending Ethiopia against the British offensive in 1941. (Public domain via Wikimedia Commons)

little doubt that, at least in part, the lack of any remarkable success on the Italian side in 1940 and the quick defeat of the Italian forces in 1941 were owed to Amedeo's weak command and leadership.

To make up for Amedeo d'Aosta's clear shortcomings, vast powers were conceded to his Chief of Staff, and Vice-Governor of Ethiopia, **Army General (Generale d'Armata) Claudio Trezzani,** who is considered the actual commander in the field of the Italian forces in East Africa. Born in 1881 in Savigliano, Trezzani attended the military academy and was commissioned in 1901 as an Alpini (mountain troops) officer. He served in the 1911–12 Italian war against Turkey and in World War I, at the end of which he was a staff officer with the rank of colonel. After teaching at the war school, he commanded a brigade in 1932 and was subsequently commander of 2 Divisione Celere (Cavalry Division). Promoted for exceptional merits to full general in 1938, Trezzani was appointed by Mussolini as Chief of Staff to the Italian command in East Africa, a position he held until the May 1941 surrender at Amba Alagi. Sent to the United States as a prisoner of war in 1944 following the Italian surrender in 1943, he became a liaison officer with the Italian co-belligerent army fighting alongside the Allies. In May 1945, he became the first Italian post-war Chief of General Staff, a position he held until 1950. He died aged 74 in 1955 in Rome.

Amedeo d'Aosta's decision to split command in East Africa in four different parts, each one practically independent, gave great powers to the individual area commanders. **General Luigi Frusci,** commander of the northern sector and governor of Eritrea, was born in 1879 at Venosa and fought in World War I, joining the Fascist Party soon after Mussolini's rise to power (this surely accounts for the lack of details about his career). A colonel in 1926, Frusci was promoted to brigadier in 1934, assigned to the War Ministry for special duties. He fought in the Italian–Ethiopian war, leading the Italian colonial troops in Somaliland (Ogaden). From 1936–37, he was in Spain fighting alongside Francisco Franco in the Spanish Civil War, before being promoted to full general in 1938. After commanding an army corps in 1939, he was sent to Ethiopia, where he was appointed governor of Amhara and, from June 1940, governor of Eritrea and commander of the Settore Nord. After surrendering following the British seizure of Eritrea, Frusci returned to Italy in 1948, being awarded Italy's most important military decoration, the Ordine Militare d'Italia (Italy's Military Order). He committed suicide in 1949, aged 70.

Commander of Scacchiere Est (Eastern Sector) was **General Guglielmo Nasi,** born in 1879 in Civitavecchia and commissioned in 1900 as an artillery officer, later attending the war school and becoming a staff officer. He took part in the Italian war against Turkey of 1911–12 and World War I as a staff officer, later being appointed Chief of Staff to the Italian command in Tripolitania (Libya). After serving as military attaché in Paris until 1928, he was appointed Chief of Staff of the Colonial troops in Cyrenaica in 1934 and at the same time was deputy governor general of the Libyan province. After commanding a division in Somaliland in 1936, he was appointed governor of Harar Governorate in 1937, becoming governor of Scioa Governorate in 1939. After leading the Italian campaign against British Somaliland, Nasi was promoted to full general and, following the British offensive, withdrew to the Gondar stronghold, where he surrendered the last organized Italian resistance on 27 November 1941. Acquitted of charges of having supported fascism, in 1949 he was given the task of supervising the handover of the colonial authority in Somaliland to the newly formed local government, but was soon compelled to resign due to protests by the Ethiopian government, which remarked that he was listed as a war criminal. He died aged 92 in 1971.

General Carlo De Simone was Nasi's leading commander in the seizure of British Somaliland. Born in 1885 in Taranto, De Simone was a Bersaglieri (light infantry) officer who took part in the 1936 Italian war against Ethiopia. Chief of Staff of the Po Army (Italy's main strategic reserve) in 1938, he commanded the armoured 'Ariete' Division before being sent to Italian East Africa, where he took command of the Truppe Harar. After the seizure of British Somaliland, De Simone was given command of part of the Juba River defences under General Gazzera. He led the withdrawal to Harar and Galla-Sidamo before surrendering and becoming a prisoner of war. After a period of command in the territorial army after the war, De Simone left the armed forces in 1950 and was appointed chief civilian administrator of Bologna (Prefetto). He died in 1951.

General Ettore Scala, commander of the Truppe Scioa, was born in 1879 and was commissioned in 1901. A lieutenant-colonel at the end of World War I, he was promoted to brigadier in 1934, taking command of an infantry brigade. A lieutenant-general in 1937, Scala was assigned to the Ministry of Colonies in the same year, being given command of the 'Granatieri di Savoia' Division in Ethiopia. Returning to Italy in 1938, Scala was put in the reserve in 1939, before being recalled and sent to East Africa to take command of the Truppe Scioa and being promoted to full general in 1940, taking over the duty of governor of Somaliland. He became a prisoner of war, but no details are available on his post-war career. His date of death is also unknown.

General Gustavo Pesenti, born in 1878, was commissioned as an Alpini officer and was soon sent to Italian Somaliland. After taking part in the Italian-Turkish war, Pesenti fought with distinction as a major in World War I and was transferred to Palestine in 1918, where he commanded the Italian contingent. Commander of the Agedabia area in Libya from 1923, he distinguished himself in the fight against the Senussi insurgency and was appointed commander of the Italian colonial troops in Somaliland in 1928. Commander of an Alpini regiment between 1929 and 1933, Pesenti was promoted to brigadier and returned to East Africa in 1935, initially as commander

General Guglielmo Nasi, who, following the defeat in Italian Somaliland, withdrew to Gondar, where he led the last large-scale Italian resistance. (senato.it, CC BY 3.0 IT, via Wikimedia Commons)

General Gustavo Pesenti, the only Italian commander in East Africa to be removed from position after the South African attack on El Wak. (Public domain via Wikimedia Commons)

of the 1st Eritrean Division and eventually as commander of the Gondar area. Promoted to major-general in 1937, he was assigned to serve again in East Africa in 1938, where he was given command of the Juba area and was governor of Italian Somaliland. Due to the failure of the defence of El Wak, which was lost to South African troops, Pesenti was removed from command and from the role of governor of Somaliland (the position being taken over by General Carlo De Simone), and he was sent back to Italy. Retired from army service immediately after repatriation, he died in 1960, aged 82.

General Pietro Gazzera was born in 1879 near Cuneo, in north-west Italy, graduating in 1898 from the Military Academy at Turin. He attended the war school in 1905 and, promoted to captain in 1910, took part in the Italian war against Turkey of 1911–12, being awarded the Silver Medal for Military Honour. A staff officer during World War I, he served first in the operations branch of the Army Staff and then with the 6th Army. Promoted to brigadier at the end of the war, Gazzera was the Italian plenipotentiary at the peace conference with Austria-Hungary. After commanding an infantry brigade, Gazzera was then deputy commander of the War School before presiding over the Turin Special Military Tribunal, acting against the anti-Fascists. Sent to Albania in 1923 to lead the commission tasked with the delimitation of the new borders, Gazzera then returned to Italy, where he took over command of the War School, being appointed by Mussolini in 1928 as Undersecretary of State at the War Ministry. This was, in fact, a promotion to leading the War Ministry since Mussolini, officially Minister of War, deputized most of the work to the undersecretaries. Made Minister of War in 1929, Gazzera was promoted to full general in 1930, soon distinguishing himself for the incorporation of the Fascist militia into the Italian Army. Gazzera was in charge until removed in 1933, after clashing with Mussolini. Made a senator (the Senate, at the time, comprised members appointed by the king), Gazzera was recalled to army duty in 1938 and was made governor of the Galla-Sidamo Governorate in East Africa. Commander of Scacchiere Sud in 1940, Gazzera succeeded Amedeo d'Aosta as Governor General of Italian East Africa and Commander-in-Chief of the Italian troops in the area following the surrender of the latter at Amba Alagi. After the defeat at Dembidollo and the withdrawal inland into Galla-Sidamo, Gazzera surrendered along with the remnants of his troops to Belgian forces on 6 July 1941. A prisoner of war first in Kenya and then in the United States, Gazzera returned to Italy following the 1943 surrender and was made High Commissioner for War Prisoners. Removed from the Senate by the post-war High Court of Justice for his cooperation with fascism, Gazzera retired from army service and died aged 73 in 1953.

General Pietro Gazzera, formerly Mussolini's deputy at the War Ministry, led the Italian forces deployed to the west of Addis Ababa until his surrender to the Belgian Force Publique on 6 July 1941. (Photo by ullstein bild via Getty Images)

OPPOSING FORCES

BRITISH

It is worth saying that, within the context of this book, the term 'British' is merely an abbreviation used to simplify and shorten the entire collection of forces and countries involved in the campaign. These actually included British, Commonwealth, Imperial and Dominion forces, which encompassed the various formations involved in the campaign and their countries of origin: India, South Africa, Sudan, Kenya, Uganda and several other countries that are today part of the Commonwealth. The East Africa campaign was mostly fought by Africans and Indians, with only a small minority of British Army units being involved in it.

After establishing the Anglo-Egyptian Condominium in Sudan following the defeat of the Mahdi's insurgency in 1899, Sudan was ruled as a colony and eventually created its own defence force. The Sudan Defence Force was in fact created in 1925, following the assassination in Cairo of the British

A camel patrol of the Sudan Defence Force, attached to 9th Indian Infantry Brigade, ready for action in the field on the Eritrean frontier near Abu Derrisa in Sudan, 1940. (Photo by No. 1 Army Film and Photo Section, AFPU/Imperial War Museums via Getty Images)

Governor General of Sudan. It was a solely British force, with British officers and senior warrant officers, mostly intended, at least in the very beginning, for use as a police and security force. Nevertheless, the Sudan Defence Force, commanded by General Sir William Platt, used Egyptian ranks and was divided into four different units: the Western Arab Corps, Eastern Arab Corps, Equatorial Corps and Camel Corps. Being spread all over Sudan, the force comprised no more than 5,000 men, with just a small, mobile elite unit (the some 500-strong Camel Corps). As such, it was hardly capable of containing an Italian invasion, even if it could also rely on the 5,000-strong French forces in French Somaliland until June 1940. The actual presence of British forces in Sudan shrank before Italy entered the war, when only three British battalions were stationed in the area (1st Worcestershire, 2nd Cheshire and 2nd York and Lancaster).

From the point of view of forces available, the situation to the north-west of Italian East Africa was matched by that in Kenya and neighbouring Uganda. Here too, a local defence force was raised, this time part of the British Army: the King's African Rifles (KAR), which distinguished itself during World War I against the German East Africa colony. Neglect and politics greatly reduced the size of the KAR and other units in the area during the inter-war period. In 1935, just as Italy was about to attack and seize Ethiopia, Britain deployed no more than 15,000 men in the Sudan and sub-Saharan area, stretching from Kenya to Rhodesia, to which South Africa could add 3,400 regular soldiers and a potential of up to 18,000 men with volunteer recruiting. In comparison, the British forces defending Egypt totalled some 23,000 men. The African units were, in most cases, little more than oversized police forces, only occasionally employed to patrol the vast borders. These units comprised the Royal West African Frontier Force, mostly recruited in the Gold Coast and Nigeria, and included the Nigeria Regiment, Sudan Defence Force and KAR, which, by 1939, had been expanded from the original three to form seven battalions for a total of 6,450 men. The creation of the Kenya Regiment in 1937 added little strength to the quite weak African forces intended to defend the British colonies and mandates.

A group of Indian soldiers from an unidentified unit at Berbera in August 1940. The Indian Army provided most of the forces involved in the East African campaign. (Australian War Memorial, P.10901.012)

French officers in French Somaliland. The Vichy French forces in the colony were not involved in the campaign, unlike the Free French ones, which distinguished themselves at Massawa. (Photo by ullstein bild via Getty Images)

The only European (to call it as such) force available was provided by South Africa, whose army was also relatively small. The South Africa Defence Force, created in 1912, was centred around a small group of regulars normally numbering no more than 2,000 men, all white since the policy was not to arm non-European (or Black) soldiers, whose duties were restricted to labour and support. In 1939, the South Africa Defence Force included a 3,350-strong permanent force plus a part-time or reserve force of 14,600 men. Mobilization of the African forces started as early as August 1939, the creation of defence forces in Uganda, Tanganyika and Nyasaland being amongst the first steps to be taken. Following the redeployment to East Africa of the West Africa troops, two brigades were formed at first, soon expanded to two divisions thanks to the addition of South African forces. After a reduction in strength mostly imposed by economic conditions following the Great Depression, this was a large expansion following the outbreak of war, with the aim of creating two infantry divisions and a 140,000-strong army. Only on 7 February 1940 were the South African soldiers asked to be ready to serve anywhere, and, following the decision to create 1st Infantry Brigade in May 1940, it soon became clear that the local European population was not enough to fill the established strength. Dealing with the issue in minimal terms, without a proper national policy, the brigade was formed, four others following in June, made with both European and African personnel. Amongst the measures taken were the creation, before the end of 1940, of a Cape Corps and an Indian Services Corps, later forming the Indian and Malay Corps, along with the creation of the Native Military Corps. Originally intended to perform only non-combat duties, the Native Military Corps was employed in a wide variety of duties and even in actual combat. After declaring war on Italy on 11 June 1940, South Africa sent 1st Brigade to Kenya, where, by the end of the year, 1st South African Division assembled. Back in the homeland, two other divisions intended to be formed were soon replaced by a Reserve Brigade composed of men not fit for front-line duties.

In January 1941, the African forces fighting against Italian East Africa included 1st South African Division, which was used to support

South African troops posing in front of a captured Italian flag at Moyale in 1941. The 1st South African Division was the most important force fighting the Italians from Kenya. (Public domain via Wikimedia Commons)

11th and 12th (African) Infantry Divisions, each one composed of an East Africa infantry brigade and a brigade from the West African colonies, respectively Nigeria and the Gold Coast. Even though it is hard to ascertain the actual number of Africans who served during World War II, both during the East African campaign and afterwards, one ought to provide a few numbers in order to remember what would otherwise be a forgotten contribution. Some 323,500 men from East Africa (largely from Kenya and Tanganyika) served mostly with the KAR units, along with some 122,000 from West Africa (generally from Nigeria and the Gold Coast) serving mostly with the Royal West African Frontier Force. To these, some 37,000 from the mandates (Basutoland, Bechuanaland and Swaziland) should be added, along with roughly 40,000 (including 10,000 Europeans) from Rhodesia. Sudan provided around 25,000 men, while the contribution of South Africa included 211,000 European and 123,000 non-European men.

Since Britain's defence needs focused first and foremost on the homeland and other strategic areas, such as the Suez Canal, there was only one source that could provide a significant contribution to the war against Italian East Africa: India. The 5th Indian Infantry Division was taken directly from the country and reached Sudan in September 1940 with a 40-ship convoy. The decision to move the 4th Indian Infantry Division, which since 9 December 1940 had been involved in Operation *Compass* against the Italians in North Africa, turned out to be a key move in the entire Mediterranean, African and Middle Eastern campaigns. The division was sent to Sudan, its first elements arriving at the end of December 1940 being accompanied by a squadron of Matilda infantry tanks from the 4th Royal Tank Regiment, which would soon prove their worth. The importance of the contribution provided by the Indian Army during the war, in particular to the victory in East Africa, cannot be stressed enough.

ITALIAN

The most important factor in evaluating the Italian forces in East Africa is their strength, which greatly surpassed that of the opposing forces. Details speak for themselves. On 1 June 1940, the *Comando Superiore Forze Armate Africa Orientale Italiana* (Italian East Africa Armed Forces High Command) had 6,114 Italian and 1,468 colonial (or African) all ranks. The colonies of Eritrea, Amhara, Ethiopia, Galla-Sidamo, Harar and Italian Somaliland had, all together, a grand total of 5,540 officers (including the Blackshirts' Fascist Militia), 5,891 non-commissioned officers, 56,510 Italian other ranks and 180,427 colonial non-commissioned officers and other ranks, for a grand total of 255,950 (rising to some 280,000 and more thanks to the further recruitment of irregular forces). To these, the police forces in the area had to be added: 9,058 Carabinieri (military police, figures including the Zaptie, or the locally recruited colonial police), 1,845 Guardia di Finanza (border control) and 6,381 Polizia Africa Italiana (Italian Africa police). This was boosted by the other armed forces, which included 10,214 with the Regia Marina (Italian Royal Navy) and 7,728 with the Regia Aeronautica.

A postcard illustrating a cavalry charge by an Italian colonial unit in the area of Lake Tana in 1941. The Italian Army relied heavily on colonial troops for the defence of East Africa. (Photo by Fireshot Studio/Fototeca/Universal Images Group via Getty Images)

Weapons included 5,313 light and 3,313 heavy machine guns, 57 light and 71 heavy mortars, 111 heavy (100mm and plus) and 700 medium field and infantry guns, 31 anti-tank and 24 anti-aircraft guns, 24 medium and 39 light tanks, 126 armoured cars and field-modified armoured trucks, 590 cars, 6,286 trucks and 988 'special' vehicles. The naval forces included one auxiliary ship, ten destroyers, five submarines and five motor torpedo boats, while the air force had at its disposal 22 bomber and five fighter groups, plus a reconnaissance unit, for a total of 183 efficient aircraft (36 fighters and 138 bombers). Clearly, the bulk of heavy weapons and artillery was used to equip the two Italian Army divisions and the other units composed by Italian nationals, leaving most of the other colonial units with only light armament and limited fighting power. Any further expansion of the Italian forces in East Africa following Italy's entry into the war was greatly limited, first by its isolation – which prevented reinforcements coming from the homeland – and secondly by the limitations imposed on local recruitment. Italian settlers were mostly employed in essential works and could not be recruited, while the shortage of officers and non-commissioned officers prevented any large-scale recruitment of African soldiers.

The Italian Army in East Africa had at its disposal a few armoured units, mostly equipped with outdated tanks like this Fiat 3000 shown during the advance on Berbera on 15 August 1940. (Photo by Weltbild/ullstein bild via Getty Images)

Poor organization was one of the main shortcomings affecting the Italian forces. These were widely dispersed in a series of units and sub-units all too often created without any apparent logic or an attempt to form effective fighting units. The two regular army divisions

were too small to provide an effective fighting force, and were actually understrength when compared with their counterparts. The 'Granatieri di Savoia' Division was a pre-existing unit with a peculiar organization only partially matching that of the homeland army. Its established strength was 8,350 all ranks, and its armament included 162 light and 104 heavy machine guns, 54 light mortars and 24 65/17 (65mm, 17-calibre) infantry guns. The 'Cacciatori d'Africa' Division was mobilized early in 1940 and had an established strength of 7,000 and armament included 25 light tanks and 26 armoured cars. The lack of fighting power affecting these two divisions, as well as most of the Italian forces, was also due to their lack of motorization and mobility. Mules, horses and camels were the basic means of transportation, motor vehicles being mostly used for supplies and made available only on request. The chaotic unit organization saw a wide variety of different formations made up of mostly locally recruited forces, which seemed to be an attempt to provide guidance to units with limited mobility, as the local forces were supposed to be better acquainted with the environment and better suited to it than their Italian counterparts.

As a result, the Italian forces in East Africa included 23 colonial brigades, raised to 29 following mobilization, each with a variable number of colonial battalions, ranging from three to five. Each one of these, usually about 800-strong, was made up of three rifle and one machine gun companies, armed with a total of 18 light and six heavy machine guns, along with two 65/17 infantry guns that were pack mounted. The rest of the Italian colonial troops formed eight Gruppo Squadrone Cavalleria (cavalry squadrons group), 22 gruppo bande and 15 independent bande (bands, irregular colonial formations each about 300-strong, with the gruppo being as much as 1,500-strong). However, any plans the Italians had for the locally recruited troops to support the formations disappeared when it became clear that such recruitment depended on local support. Most African soldiers were followed by a 'family camp', which, while assuring the loyalty and even bravery of the African soldiers, prevented them from moving too far away from their homes or fighting for prolonged periods of time. As soon as the Italians were driven away from their positions, their 'Ascari' (the Askari, African soldiers) tended to desert to return to their families and places of origin.

BELOW LEFT
German nationals living in Abyssinia, along with the crews of German ships that sought sanctuary in the Ethiopian harbours, formed a unit that fought alongside the Italians in Eritrea. They are shown wearing Italian uniforms and webbing with homemade insignia. (Photo by ullstein bild via Getty Images)

BELOW RIGHT
The handing out of the German company pennant in October 1940. The Germans formed a quasi-independent unit that was considered a volunteer formation part of the Italian Army. (Photo by Weltbild/ ullstein bild via Getty Images)

ORDERS OF BATTLE

BRITISH

MIDDLE EAST COMMAND, 1940

Commander-in-Chief MEC – General Sir Archibald Wavell
General Officer Commanding Troops in the Sudan – Major-General
William Platt
1st Worcestershire Regiment
1st Essex Regiment
2nd West Yorkshire Regiment
Sudan Defence Force (21 companies from Camel Corps, Eastern
Arab Corps, Western Arab Corps)

**General Officer Commanding East Africa Force – Major-General
Douglas Dickinson**
Southern Brigade/1st Brigade King's African Rifles (KAR),
Brigadier Charles Christopher Fowkes
Northern Brigade/2nd Brigade KAR, Brigadier Colin Frederick
Blackden
East African Reconnaissance Regiment, subsequently 1st East
African Armoured Car Regiment
22nd (Derajat) Mountain Battery, Frontier Force

On 30 July, the following reorganization was envisaged:
Reorganization of 1st (East African) Brigade (1/4th KAR, 2/4th
KAR, 2/6th KAR)
Creation of:
5th (East African) Brigade (2/1st KAR, 2/2nd KAR, 3/6th KAR)
6th (East African) Brigade (2/3rd KAR, 3/4th KAR, 4/4th KAR)

On 17 October, the following changes took place:
1st (EA) Brigade and 3rd Nigerian Brigade were to form the
Coastal Division, 1st Brigade became 21st (EA) Brigade forming
1st (Africa) Division
2nd (EA) Brigade and 4th Gold Coast Brigade were to form the
Northern Frontier District (NFD) Division, 2nd Brigade became
22nd (EA) Brigade forming 2nd (Africa) Division
3rd (Nigeria) Brigade became 23rd (Nigerian) Brigade forming
the 1st (Africa) Division
4th (Gold Coast) Brigade became 24th (Gold Coast) Brigade

**British Somaliland Forces – Lieutenant-Colonel Arthur Reginald
Chater (Major-General Reade Godwin-Austen from 11 August 1940)**
Somaliland Camel Corps
1st Northern Rhodesia Regiment
2nd (Nyasaland) King's African Rifles
3/15th Punjab Regiment (since 1 July)
1/2nd Punjab Regiment (since 7 August)
2nd Black Watch (since 8 August)
1st East African Light Battery

MIDDLE EAST COMMAND, 1941

Commander-in-Chief MEC – General Sir Archibald Wavell
British Troops in the Sudan – Lieutenant-General William Platt
Directly subordinated:
B Squadron, 4th Royal Tank Regiment
Sudan Defence Force
Mission 101 (related to Gideon Force)
2/5th Mahratta Light Infantry (see 4th Indian Infantry Division)
2/6th King's African Rifles
51st (Middle East) Commando
52nd Commando
Sudan Defence Force
1st Independent anti-tank group
68th Medium Regiment Royal Artillery

**4th Indian Infantry Division – Major-General Noel Beresford-
Peirse**
5th Indian Infantry Brigade, Brigadier Wilfrid Lewis Lloyd
(1st Royal Fusiliers, 3/1st Punjab Regiment, 4/6th [Outram's]
Rajputana Rifles)
7th Indian Infantry Brigade, Brigadier Harold Rawdon Briggs
(1st Royal Sussex Regiment, 4/11th Sikh Regiment, 4/16th
[Bhopal] Punjab Regiment)
11th Indian Infantry Brigade, Brigadier Reginald Savory
(2nd Queen's Own Cameron Highlanders, 1/6th [Wellesley's]
Rajputana Rifles, 3/14th Punjab Regiment; attached on
11 February 1941: 2/5th Mahratta Light Infantry)
Central India Horse (21st King George V's Own Horse)
1st, 25th, 31st Field Regiment Royal Artillery
Gazelle Force, Colonel Frank Messervy (formed 16 October 1940,
disbanded 13 February 1941 from Skinner's Horse [1st Duke of
York's Own Cavalry]), units attached included:
1st Duke of York's Own Skinner's Horse
4/11th Sikh Regiment
Three motorized machine-gun companies from the Sudan Defence
Force
390th (Sussex Yeomanry) Field Battery, 144th Field Regiment Royal
Artillery

5th Indian Infantry Division – Major-General Lewis Heath
9th Indian Infantry Brigade, Brigadier Mosley Mayne, since 1 March
1941 Brigadier Frank Messervy, since 13 April 1941 Brigadier
Bernard Fletcher
(2nd West Yorkshire Regiment [Prince of Wales' Own], 3/5th
Mahratta Light Infantry, 3rd [Royal Sikhs]/12th Frontier Force
Regiment)
10th Indian Infantry Brigade, Brigadier William Slim, since 21 January
1941 Lieutenant-Colonel Bernard Fletcher, since 21 March 1941
Brigadier Thomas Rees
(1st Essex Regiment [replaced on 22 December 1940 by
2nd Highland Light Infantry (City of Glasgow)], 4th [Duke of
Connaught's Own]/10th Baluch Regiment, 3/18th Royal Garhwal
Rifles)
29th Indian Infantry Brigade, Brigadier John Marriott
(1st Worcestershire Regiment, 3/2nd Punjab, 6/13th Frontier
Force Rifles)
1st Duke of York's Own Skinner's Horse
4th, 28th, 144th Field Regiment Royal Artillery

Briggs Force, Brigadier Harold Rawdon Briggs
1st Royal Sussex Regiment
4/16th (Bhopal) Punjab Regiment
Free France Brigade d'Orient, Colonel Ralph Monclar (1er Bataillon
Legion Etrangere, Bataillon de Marche 3 [Tirailleurs Senegalais],
3e companie 1er Bataillon Infanterie de Marine, 1er escadron
Spahis Marocains, 1er groupe artillerie coloniale)

Gideon Force, Colonel Orde Wingate
Sudan Defence Force Frontier Battalion
2nd Ethiopian Battalion

East Africa Force – Lieutenant-General Alan Cunningham
Directly subordinated:
1st East African Armoured Car Regiment
1st South African Light Tank Company
Somaliland Camel Corps
1/3rd King's African Rifles

1st South African Infantry Division – Major-General George Brink

2nd South African Infantry Brigade, Brigadier F. L. A. Buchanan
(1st Field Force, 2nd Field Force, 1st Natal Mounted Rifles)

5th South African Infantry Brigade, Brigadier Bertram Armstrong
(1st [South African] Irish Regiment, 2nd Regiment Botha, 3rd Transvaal Scottish)

25th (East Africa) Brigade, Brigadier W. Owen (attached on 28 December 1940 from 12th [African] Infantry Division and detached on 19 September 1941)
(2/3rd King's African Rifles, 2/4th King's African Rifles)

3rd South African Field Brigade (Transvaal Horse Artillery), 4th South African Field Brigade, 1st South African Anti-Tank Brigade

11th (African) Infantry Division – Major-General Harry Wetherall

21st (East Africa) Infantry Brigade, Brigadier Alan MacDougall Ritchie
(detached on 27 February to 1st South African Division)
(1/2nd King's African Rifles, 1/4th King's African Rifles, 1st Northern Rhodesia Regiment)

23rd (Nigeria) Infantry Brigade, Brigadier Gerald Smallwood
(1st, 2nd, 3rd Nigeria Regiment, Royal West African Frontier Force)

26th (East African) Brigade, Brigadier William Dimoline (detached from division)
(2/2nd, 3/6th, 4/4th King's African Rifles)

C Squadron, 1st East African Armoured Car Regiment
7th South African Field Brigade, South African Artillery

12th (African) Infantry Division – Major-General Godwin-Austen

1st South African Infantry Brigade, Brigadier Dan Pienaar (brigade was detached to 12th Division until 7 March, then to 11th [African] Division until 9 May, then to 5th Indian Division until 22 May)
(1st Royal Natal Carabineers, 1st Duke of Edinburgh's Own Rifles, 1st Transvaal Scottish)

22nd (East Africa) Infantry Brigade, Brigadier Charles Christopher Fowkes, since 3 March 1941 Lieutenant-Colonel Colin Frederick Blackden
(1/1st King's African Rifles, 5th King's African Rifles, 1/6th King's African Rifles)

24th (Gold Coast) Infantry Brigade, Brigadier Collen Edward Melville Richards
(1st, 2nd, 3rd Gold Coast Regiment, Royal West African Frontier Force)

B Squadron, 1st East African Armoured Car Regiment
4th South African Field Brigade, South African Artillery

British Somaliland Forces, Brigadier Arthur Reginald Chater (from Aden)

1/2nd Punjab Regiment
3/15th Punjab Regiment
Somaliland Camel Corps

ITALIAN

COMANDO FORZE ARMATE AFRICA ORIENTALE ITALIANA, 10 June 1940

Commander-in-Chief: Generale Armata Aerea (General) HRH Prince Amedeo di Savoia Aosta, Viceroy of Ethiopia
Directly subordinated:
Gruppo artiglieria motorizzata IV, XXV, XXVI, XXXI, XXXII, CII, CIII, CIV, CV, CVI (motorised artillery bns)

Scacchiere Nord – Lieutenant-General Luigi Frusci

Directly subordinated:
XVI Brigata Coloniale (Colonel Manlio Manetti)
Col Bns (Colonial Battalions) XXII, XXIII, XLVII, LIII; Col Art Bn XVI; Col Cav Sq 16
XLI Brigata Coloniale (Brigadier Ugo Fongoli)
Col Bns XCVIII, XCIX, CXXXI, CXXXII; Col Art Bn XLI; Col Cav Sq 41

Truppe Eritrea, Major-General Vincenzo Tessitore
V Brigata Coloniale (Brigadier Angelo Bergonzi)
Col Bns XCVII, CV, CVI; Col Art Bn V; Col Cav Sqn 5
VIII Brigata Coloniale (Colonel Antonio Rizzo)
Col Bns CI, CII; Col Art Bn VIII; Col Cav Sqn 8
XII Brigata Coloniale (Colonel Ugo Tabellini)
Col Bns XXXV, XXXVI, XLIII; Col Art Bn XII; Col Cav Sqn 12
2 Legione CCNN 'Ivo Oliveti'
CCNN Bns XIII, XIV, XVI, CXVI; one col art bn

Truppe Hamara, Major-General Agostino Martini
Directly subordinated:
Battaglioni Coloniali III, CVIII, CXIV
1 and 2 Gruppo Bande
III Brigata Coloniale (Colonel Saverio Maraventano)
Col Bns XI, XXIII, XXX, LXX; Col Art Bn III; Col Cav Sqn 3
IV Brigata Coloniale (Colonel Livio Bonelli)
Col Bns XIV, XXV, XXVII, XXIX; Col Art Bn IV; Col Cav Sqn 4
XIX Brigata Coloniale (Colonel Enrico Durante)
Col Bns XXI, LXV, LXXII, LXXXVI; Col Art Bn XIX; Col Cav Sqn 19
XXI Brigata Coloniale (Colonel Ignazio Angelini)
Col Bns LXXVII, LXXVIII, LXXIX, LXXX; Col Art Bn XXI; Col Cav Sqn 21

XXII Brigata Coloniale (Colonel Adriano Torelli)
Col Bns LXVII, LXVIII, LXIX, LXXXI; Col Art Bn XXII; Col Cav Sqn 22
3 Legione CCNN 'Reginaldo Giuliani'
CCNN Bns CXXXI, CXLI, CXLVI, CLI
7 Legione CCNN 'F. Battisti'
CCNN Bns CLXV, CCXL, DCXXX, DCXXXV

Scacchiere Est – Lieutenant-General Guglielmo Nasi

Directly subordinated:
Battaglione carri M (medium tanks bn)
Battaglione carri L (light tanks bn)

(At disposal, subordinated to Comando Forze Armate AOI)
65 Divisione 'Granatieri di Savoia', Brigadier Amadeo Liberati
10 Reggimento Granatieri (two Granatieri bns, Battaglione Alpini 'Uork Amba')
11 Reggimento Granatieri (two Granatieri bns, Bersaglieri d'Africa bn)
Battaglione mitraglieri
60 Reggimento Artiglieria (five bns)
XI Legione CCNN (CCNN bns I, XII)
Gruppo Squadroni Cavalleria 'Neghelli' (two cavalry sqn)

(At disposal, subordinated to Comando Forze Armate AOI)
40 Divisione Cacciatori d'Africa
210 Reggimento Fanteria (two bns)
211 Reggimento Fanteria (two bns)
III/X Battaglione CCNN
XV/X Battaglione CCNN
XVIII Battaglione misto genio d'Africa
Gruppo artiglieria motorizzato d'Africa (mot art bn)
Added:
Gruppo battaglioni CCNN d'Africa (four bns)
Battaglione mitraglieri CCNN d'Africa

II Brigata Coloniale (Colonel Orlando Lorenzini)
Col Bns IV, V, IX, X; Col Art Bn II; Col Cav Sqn 2
VI Brigata Coloniale (Colonel Agostino Magrini)
Col Bns XIX, XXIV, XXXI, XXXIV; Col Art Bn V; Col Cav Sqn 6
VII Brigata Coloniale (Colonel Tiburzio Rean)

Col Bns XIII, XV, XLV; Col Art Bn VII; Col Cav Sqn 7
XI Brigata Coloniale (Colonel Francesco Prina)
    Col Bns LI, LII, LVI; Col Art Bn XI; Col Cav Sqn 11

Truppe Harar, Major-General Carlo De Simone
Directly subordinated:
XIV Gruppo Squadroni Cavalleria Coloniale
Squadrone Autoblindo (armoured cars)
XIII Brigata Coloniale (Brigadier Cesare Nam)
    Col Bns XX, XXXIX, XLVIII; Col Art Bn XIII; Col Cav Sqn 13
XIV Brigata Coloniale (Colonel Siliprandi)
    Col Bns XXXVII, LXIV, LXXXIII; Col Art Bn XIV; Col Cav Sqn 14
XV Brigata Coloniale (Major Romano)
    Col Bns XXXVIII, XL, XLIX, CXLII; Col Art Bn XV; Col Cav Sqn 15
XVII Brigata Coloniale (Colonel Focanti)
    Col Bns XLII, LVIII, LXVI; Col Art Bn XVII; Col Cav Sqn 17
4 Legione CCNN 'Filippo Corridoni'
    CCNN Bns CLXIV, CLXVI, DII, DIV

Truppe Scioa, Lieutenant-General Ettore Scala
Directly subordinated:
Gruppo Squadroni Cavalleria Coloniale I, II, III, V, XV
XX Brigata Coloniale (Colonel Giuseppe Azzolini)*
    Col Bns XL, LXXIV, LXXV, LXXVI; Col Art Bn XX; Col Cav Sqn 20
(*forming the 101 Divisione Coloniale)
XXIII Brigata Coloniale (Lieutenant-Colonel Casabassa)
    Col Bns LXXXVIII, LXXXIX, XC; Col Art Bn XXIII; Col Cav Sqn 23
1 Legione CCNN 'Arnaldo Mussolini'
    CCNN Bns II, IV, V, XI
Comando Addis Abeba
(with two CCNN AA bns, two heavy field artillery bns, two position
    heavy artillery bns)

**Settore Autonomo Giuba, Lieutenant-General Gustavo Pesenti
(from 1 January 1941 Scacchiere)**
Directly subordinated:
Battaglioni costieri coloniali IV, V (coastal colonial bns)
Gruppo artiglieria coloniale CI (artillery bn)
Raggruppamento coloniale di frontiera (border colonial bn)
Raggruppamento Dubat with Dubat unit groups I–V
XCI Brigata Coloniale (Colonel Italo Carnevali)
    Col Bns LXXV, CXCIV, CXCVI; Col Art Bn XCI; Col Cav Sqn 91
(forming the 102 Divisione Coloniale)
XCII Brigata Coloniale (Colonel Giaume)*
    Col Bns LXXIV, CXCI, CXCII; Col Art Bn XCII; Col Cav Sqn 92
(*forming the 101 Divisione Coloniale)
5 Legione CCNN 'Luigi Razza'
    CCNN Bns DV, DVI, DLXXXV, DCXXXI

Scacchiere Sud, Lieutenant-General Pietro Gazzera
Directly subordinated:
Gruppo Squadroni cavalleria coloniale VI, XI
Gruppo Artiglieria Contraerea CCNN (anti-aircraft bn)
Raggruppamento coloniale di frontiera (border colonial bn) III, IV, V
LXXXV Brigata Coloniale
    Col Bns CLXXXIII, CLXXXIV, CLXXXV, CLXXXVI; Col Art Bn LXXXV;
    Col Cav Sqn 85

Comando Truppe Galla e Sidama – Lieutenant-General Pietro
    Gazzera
I Brigata Coloniale (Colonel Guido Pialorsi)
    Col Bns I, VI, VIII, XVIII; Col Art Bn III; Col Cav Sqn 1
IX Brigata Coloniale (Colonel Flaminio Orrigo)
    Col Bns II, XVII, LIX, LX; Col Art Bn IX; Col Cav Sqn 9
X Brigata Coloniale (Colonel Giuseppe Cloza)
    Col Bns XXVIII, L, CLXXXI, CLXXXVII; Col Art Bn X; Col Cav Sqn 10
XVIII Brigata Coloniale (Colonel Bartolomeo Minola)
    Col Bns XVI, LXI, CLXXXII, CXXXLIII; Col Art Bn XVIII; Col Cav Sqn
    18
XXV Brigata Coloniale (Lieutenant-Colonel Giorgio Rolandi)

Col Bns VII, XXVIII, LIV; Col Art Bn XXV; Col Cav Gp 25
6 Legione CCNN 'Luigi Valcarenghi'
    CCNN Bns DCCXXXI, XCCXLV

In June 1940, the following Divisione Coloniale (colonial divisions)
    were supposed to be formed with the listed units, but their
    actual formation is unclear:
Divisione Coloniale Harar (Brigata Coloniale XIII, XV, XIX)
1 Divisione Eritrea (Brigata Coloniale V, XLIV)
2 Divisione Eritrea (Brigata Coloniale VIII, XVI)
21 Divisione Coloniale (Brigata Coloniale IX, XVIII)
22 Divisione Coloniale (Brigata Coloniale I, LXXXVI)
23 Divisione Coloniale (Brigata Coloniale X)

OPPOSING PLANS

BRITISH

British pre-war strategy for the region merely aimed at isolating Italian East Africa in order to deprive the area of reinforcements and supplies and also to deny any opportunity to harass the Red Sea naval routes. A possible offensive aimed at Addis Ababa was considered, starting from the French colony of French Somaliland and necessarily relying on reinforcements from the homeland. These labile intentions, overturned by the French defeat in June 1940, were transformed into a coherent strategy thanks to General Archibald Wavell, General Officer Commander-in-Chief Middle East since August 1939. Facing overwhelmingly superior enemy forces (the Italians had some half a million troops in Libya and East Africa, while Wavell had just 30,000 or so men in Egypt, Palestine and Sudan, plus some 10,000 in Kenya and British Somaliland, the overall figure rising to a total of some 47,000 by June 1940), Wavell planned to confuse and surprise the enemy as to where the British forces might attack. Acting upon Whitehall's order, Wavell focused on the defence of British possessions, trying to avoid any provocative move against Italy which might lead to a reaction. The result was a strategic bluff intended to show more strength and forces than actually existed. It worked, thanks also to Italian ineptitude, and Wavell secured first and foremost what was Britain's most important strategic position in the entire area: Egypt.

Having secured Egypt, Wavell's next step was to think of East Africa. His approach to this matter must be understood, as it was quite peculiar. Wavell saw East Africa not as an isolated area separated from the rest of the Mediterranean and the Middle East, but rather as the left flank of his whole front, which was North Africa. As such, Wavell did not consider what could have been a viable strategic alternative, which was to permanently isolate East Africa and starve it by using the barest minimum of forces, but instead aimed from the very beginning at the eradication of the Italian presence in the area. Wavell outlined his plans for East Africa in October 1939, planning a strike from the north but also taking into account an advance from the south, both of which required the necessary support and troops suitably trained to deal with both terrain and climate. This was in conjunction with waging irregular warfare in order to not just try to restore Emperor Haile Selassie's rule over Ethiopia but also as a means to split Italian control, dividing Ethiopia from Italian Somaliland. In 1939, Wavell's aggressive strategy was not welcomed by the Joint Planning Staff in Cairo, which even went so far as questioning the actual value of an offensive against Italian East Africa.

The British failure to defend Somaliland in August 1940 was followed in September by the short-lived Italian offensive into Egypt, both of which showed how precarious Wavell's position was. A less determined commander might have chosen to defend what he could, but Wavell started preparations to attack in both North and East Africa, right at a time when Britain itself still faced the threat of invasion. As far as East Africa was concerned, Wavell had a clear view: the Italians had resources barely sufficient to hold for one year, which would be quickly exhausted if facing an enemy offensive. There was thus a chance to achieve a swift victory in East Africa that would free the necessary forces to defend and counter-attack in North Africa. A decisive role would be played by South Africa and its political and military leadership, which opposed Italy and its expansionism. The outline of the basic plan, now aimed at attacking Italian Somaliland, was drafted during the 29 October conference in Khartoum, and the appointment of General Cunningham in command in Kenya provided the first step towards the offensive. The final step was given by the arrival in Sudan of the 5th Indian Division, the actual offensive starting soon after.

There is one crucial decision which, according to some, was to influence the North and East African campaigns: Wavell's decision to withdraw the 4th Indian Division from Egypt and send it to Sudan. It is arguable whether General O'Connor might have continued his advance into Libya, reaching Tripoli before the arrival of the Afrika Korps, had the division not been transferred, but Wavell's decision certainly contributed to the swift victory in East Africa, which would soon prove to be a determinant in the war fought in an area stretching from the Balkans to East Africa itself.

ITALIAN

Two factors influenced the Italian war plans for East Africa. The first was the local insurgency, which the Italians had been fighting since 1936 without success, its main achievement being mostly psychological. Facing

An Italian colonial unit returning to Addis Ababa after the Italian conquest of British Somaliland in September 1940. The Italian Army still widely used cavalry formations, which although effective did not increase its mobility. (Photo by Weltbild/ullstein bild via Getty Images)

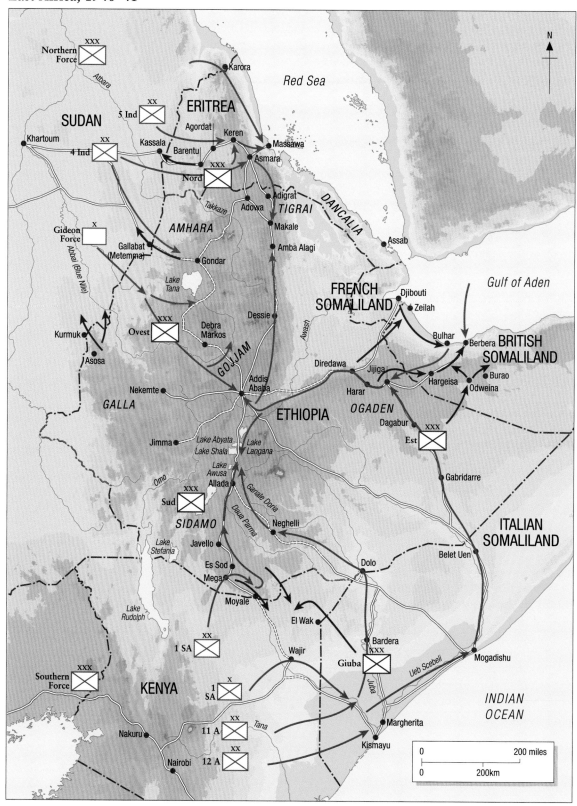

the British offensive and the ever-growing Arbegnoch insurgency, the Italians were practically paralyzed by the latter, which they felt unable to control. The second factor was the basic consideration that, owing to the superiority of the French and British naval forces, no reinforcements or even supplies could be brought to Italy's African colonies once at war. Any possibility that a strategic plan focusing on Africa, and especially on a double offensive from North and East Africa, could materialize disappeared in 1937 when the Italian Navy Staff made the situation clear. Mussolini's pre-war directives thus focused on limited offensives from East Africa, mostly directed against positions near the border or against French Somaliland (Italy's main aim) and British Somaliland, without ever considering that by lacking a strategic overall plan, the fate of his 'Empire' would be doomed from the beginning of the war.

A local factor that would exercise an even greater influence on the Italian war planning was the amateurish and unimaginative command of Amedeo d'Aosta. There was no Paul Lettow-Vorbeck in Italian East Africa, no commander capable of conceiving a sort of war that could keep the enemy at bay while harassing his positions, as the German general had done during World War I. The actual Italian defence plan was catastrophically simple: to defend the Italian possessions all along the borders with a minimum of force. The limited reserves, mostly the two army divisions, were to be used to plug any gap created by the enemy offensives and were deployed in Eritrea. Only in 1938 did General Ugo Cavallero suggest a defence aimed at preserving control of Eritrea and Massawa as long as possible in order to interdict the Red Sea and the Nile. His removal put an end to this idea, leading to a static defence that lacked completely any sort of fortifications and depth. Once the defence lines along the border were broken through, the Italians, lacking reserves, no longer possessed the means to deal with the enemy penetration. The result was that entire regions, as in the case of the Juba River, had to be abandoned practically without a fight.

As soon as the Italian positions along the borders collapsed, any centralized command effectively disappeared. Local commands, which always enjoyed a great deal of independence from the Comando Superiore, were tied down by their actual deployments and by the lack of mobility of their African units, with the result that each one focused on the defence of its own areas without any attempt at coordination or at developing an alternative strategy. The obvious consequence was that the Italians proved unable to defend their own territories, Eritrea and Somaliland, and were forced to withdraw into the least accessible areas of Ethiopia, where they formed their last redoubts. One crucial factor must be taken into account before anything else: the sheer size of the battlefield. Ethiopia alone is almost 1,500km long and 1,200km wide (Eritrea and Somaliland added almost half of these figures again), which is about the same size as France and Italy combined. Even though operations were mostly restricted to key areas, especially crucial communications centres, the Italians relied on the sheer size of their East African possession to be able to resist in their redoubts for a long period of time, defying an enemy whose movements would be hindered by terrain and climate. Such a strategy did not take into account the fact that, practically isolated in a hostile country and environment, the eradication of these redoubts could only be a matter of time and that their actual presence was irrelevant anyhow.

THE CAMPAIGN

THE ITALIANS ON THE OFFENSIVE, JUNE–AUGUST 1940

Following Italy's entry into the war on 10 June 1940, military activities in East Africa were limited. The Royal Air Force started a series of air raids that found the Italians unprepared. At the same time, Italian forces on the borders started a series of raids and *coups de main* aimed at gaining information and details on the enemy troops they were facing. This was, at least in part, due to the uncertain situation of French Somaliland, which was a key area in the Italian pre-war planning. On one side, the Italians planned on seizing French Somaliland by force, which required a pretext since the territory, according to the armistice treaty when France surrendered in 1940, was to be demilitarized and its facilities made available for use by the Italians. The initial anti-Axis attitude of French governor General Legentilhomme suggested that French Somaliland might not adhere to the armistice but rather try to join General de Gaulle's pro-Britain movement. Minor clashes took place at the border until, on 19 July, General Germain, sent by the Vichy government, took over, assuring French Somaliland's loyalty and compelling the British forces to withdraw. By 28 July, the situation had been stabilized, and while Legentilhomme defected to the British, the Italians had to face the fact that a military seizure of French Somaliland was no longer possible. As a consequence, all the Italians could now seize by force were the British positions along the borders with East Africa and, above all, British Somaliland.

In July, Mussolini decided to wait before undertaking any action in view of the possible developments in Europe. Meanwhile, in East Africa, Amedeo D'Aosta had to deal with the fact that the majority of the forces available (about 90–100 colonial battalions) were tied up in the interior dealing with the Ethiopian insurgency, and the few

Italian colonial troops attacking a village near Kurmuk (Sudan) in late summer 1940. (Photo by ullstein bild via Getty Images)

modern, mobile forces were concentrated in the Scioa and Harar regions, waiting for a clarification of the situation in French Somaliland. Considering the imminence of the rainy season, any possibility for a large-scale offensive operation against Sudan and Kenya was excluded once and for all, leaving only small-scale operations. These aimed at the seizure of the border towns of Kassala, Gallabat and Kurmuk in Sudan, and of Moyale in Kenya. Kurmuk, considered valuable by the Italians, became even more important following the series of raids carried out beyond the Italian frontier by the Sudan Defence Force.

Italian troop concentration on the border with British Somaliland in the days before the invasion. (Photo by ullstein bild via Getty Images)

The seizure of Kassala was considered particularly important by Amedeo D'Aosta, who saw in it the possibility to improve the defences of Eritrea and pave the way for any future operation in Sudan. The task was given to General Tessitore, commander of troops in Eritrea, and it turned out to be a rather easy one. Kassala was attacked on 4 July by two columns totalling 4,800 colonial troops and 1,500 cavalrymen, supported by two artillery battalions, three medium and three light tanks. The defenders, two companies of the Sudan Defence Force – No. 5 Motor Machine Gun Company and No. 6 Mounted Infantry Company – managed to face the attack with minimal losses (ten in all), inflicting the loss of 117 Italians while withdrawing and reassembling north of the town. On that same day, a colonial banda drove away No. 3 Company of the Eastern Arab Corps from Gallabat, while Karora and Kurmuk, both on the Sudanese border, were seized after small skirmishes against the local police forces.

The same kind of action took place along the Kenyan border, where Italian forces seized Moyale on 10 July, successfully repulsing a series of counter-attacks on the 15th, when a series of attacks from Italian Somaliland and Ethiopia granted the Italians control of the Buna salient, the stretch of Kenyan territory wedged in between the aforementioned territories. With the start of the rainy season at the end of July impeding any further activity in Sudan, the Italians turned towards British Somaliland. This was because its seizure would eradicate a potential threat from the north-east, while at the same time easing the defence of the area, and also because the attack was intended to divert attention and resources from the offensive that was intended to start in North Africa.

The Italian attack plan was marred from the start by inaccurate maps that misled which was the most suitable road to use for approaching Tug Argan and, from there, reaching Berbera. Facing an estimated 11,000 enemy troops, the Italians prepared an operational corps commanded by General Nasi, which included a total of 26 battalions (23 of which were colonial troops) and 21 field gun batteries for a combined 4,800 Italian and 30,000 colonial troops supported by medium tanks and 27 bomber, 23 fighter and seven reconnaissance aircraft. The bulk of the Italian forces was made up by the Colonna di Centro (central column) under the orders of General de Simone, with the Divisione Speciale Harar (Harar Special Division) with three colonial brigades totalling 11 battalions and 14 gun batteries. Its aim

Italian troops marching past a well in British Somaliland in August 1940. They all wear the standard Italian colonial uniform with trousers, shirtsleeve order and a blanket rolled around their chest. (Photo by Weltbild/ullstein bild via Getty Images)

was to move from Jijiga and advance along the main route in order to reach Berbera. The attack also included a Colonna di Sinistra (left column), which was to advance from Aysha to reach the coast at Zeilah. Once Zeilah had been seized, the Colonna Costiera (coastal column) was to advance along the coast, reaching Bulhar, to the west of Berbera. To the east, the Colonna di Destra (right column) was to advance across the desert to Odweina and, from there, move to the east towards Burao and to the west to join the Colonna di Centro at the Tug Argan Pass, where British forces were supposed to defend the approaches to Berbera. The seizure of Berbera was deemed to be the key to the whole of Somaliland, any other objective being considered of minor or even no importance. Preparations included troops being moved from areas as far as 1,000km away, with the aim of overwhelming the British defences at Tug Argan, which were deemed to be well-manned and prepared.

Before the Italian attack started, General Wavell examined the situation with the local commander, Lieutenant-Colonel (soon promoted to Brigadier) Chater, coming to the conclusion that no fewer than five battalions would be needed in order to have a chance to deal with the Italians. At the beginning of August, Chater had at his disposal four battalions, which would be joined on 7 August by the 2nd Black Watch from Aden, one light gun battery with 3.7in howitzers and a reinforcement of 17 officers and 20 non-commissioned officers from Southern Rhodesia. Each one of these units, being composed of different races, required special treatment and food and they were bound to act independently, since no organized headquarters was available. The Aden Air Force provided the only air support, and two 3in guns from the 23rd Battery Royal Artillery from Aden were the only reinforcement. The disparity of forces, soon to become evident, made the defence of the Tug Argan Pass (Tug meaning torrent) the crucial position to prevent the fall of Berbera, which, in any case, could hardly be avoided in the long run.

An Italian motorized column advancing into British Somaliland in August 1940. In the centre are two outdated Lancia armoured cars. (Photo by Weltbild/ullstein bild via Getty Images)

Italian conquest of British Somaliland, 4 August 1940

BRITISH
British Somaliland Forces – Brigadier Arthur Reginald Chater RM (also CO Somaliland Camel Corps)
Somaliland Camel Corps
1st Northern Rhodesia Regiment
2nd King's African Rifles (Nyasaland)
1st East African Light Battery
1/2nd Punjab Regiment
3/15th Punjab Regiment
2nd Black Watch (since 7 August)

ITALIAN
Corpo di Operazione (operational corps) – Lieutenant-General Guglielmo Nasi
Colonna di Sinistra (left column, General Bertoldi)
LXX Brigata Coloniale, XVII Brigata Coloniale (total: five colonial battalions, two CCNN and one machine guns from the 'Granatieri di Savoia', plus 21 gun batteries)
Colonna Costiera (coastal column, General Passerone)
One CCNN and one colonial battalions
Colonna di Centro (central column, General De Simone)
Divisione Speciale Harar comprising XIII, XIV, XV Brigata Coloniale, 322 Compagnia Carri M, Compagnia Carri Veloci 'Cavalieri di Neghelli' (total: 11 colonial battalions, 14 gun batteries, medium and light tanks companies)
Colonna di Destra (right column, General Bertello)
One Arab–Somali battalion, two Dubat groups
Riserva del comando (command reserve force, General Lorenzini)
II Brigata Coloniale (total: four colonial battalions, two gun batteries)

The Italian attack started on 3 August, with the units approaching the border and, in some cases, crossing it without facing much opposition. By the 5th, the left column had reached the coast at Zeilah, the central column had advanced to Hargeisa and the right column made it to Odweina, closing in to Berbera. On 7 August, Nasi ordered the Divisione Speciale Harar to advance along the main road to Berbera, while the Colonna di Destra (which on the next day would be absorbed by the Colonna di Centro) was to move from Odweina to Adadle. In the meantime, the reserves were to reach a position to the left of the Colonna di Centro, preparing to attack the British positions. The Italian advance, albeit steady, lacked vigour and enabled Brigadier Chater to hold up the Colonna di Centro at Hargeisa with the Camel Corps, supported by a company of the Northern Rhodesia Regiment. This, along with the Italians' lack of accurate maps, slowed down the advance, which only reached the Tug Argan Pass on 10 August, giving time for General Wavell to reinforce the Somaliland defences with field and anti-tank artillery, the defenders having noticed the presence of tanks amongst the attackers. Given the increased number of units in the area, Wavell also appointed Major-General Godwin-Austen, who arrived at Berbera on the 11th, in command, with the task of defending Berbera but also to prepare the evacuation. As Godwin-Austen arrived at Berbera, the Colonna di Centro attacked Tug

BELOW LEFT
An Italian supply column with camels on the way to the Kenyan border town of Moyale in August 1940. (Photo by ullstein bild via Getty Images)

BELOW RIGHT
Italian light trucks advancing across the desert on their way towards Berbera on 10 August 1940. (Photo by Weltbild/ullstein bild via Getty Images)

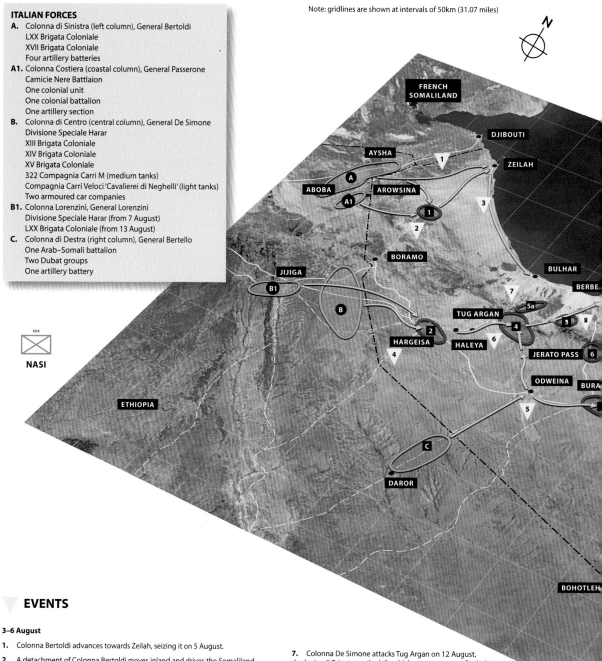

ITALIAN FORCES

A. Colonna di Sinistra (left column), General Bertoldi
LXX Brigata Coloniale
XVII Brigata Coloniale
Four artillery batteries

A1. Colonna Costiera (coastal column), General Passerone
Camicie Nere Battlaion
One colonial unit
One colonial battalion
One artillery section

B. Colonna di Centro (central column), General De Simone
Divisione Speciale Harar
XIII Brigata Coloniale
XIV Brigata Coloniale
XV Brigata Coloniale
322 Compagnia Carri M (medium tanks)
Compagnia Carri Veloci 'Cavalierei di Neghelli' (light tanks)
Two armoured car companies

B1. Colonna Lorenzini, General Lorenzini
Divisione Speciale Harar (from 7 August)
LXX Brigata Coloniale (from 13 August)

C. Colonna di Destra (right column), General Bertello
One Arab–Somali battalion
Two Dubat groups
One artillery battery

Note: gridlines are shown at intervals of 50km (31.07 miles)

NASI

▼ EVENTS

3–6 August

1. Colonna Bertoldi advances towards Zeilah, seizing it on 5 August.

2. A detachment of Colonna Bertoldi moves inland and drives the Somaliland Camel Corps company away from the area of Dobo.

3. Colonna Passerone reaches the coast near Zeilah before turning eastward and advancing towards Berbera. On 17 August, the column reaches Bulhar but is unable to advance further due to poor road conditions.

4. Colonna De Simone seizes Hargeisa on 5 August, enabling Colonna Lorenzini to approach the main road to Berbera.

5. Colonna Bertello advances to Odweina, which is taken before the column moves onto Burao, which is reached on 6 August. At this point, the column is ordered to send LXX Brigata west towards the Tug Argan Pass.

7–15 August

6. On 7 August, Divisione Speciale Harar moves from Hargeisa, followed, on the 9th, by a *colonna di formazione* ('provisional column') made of II and LXX Brigata, XIII, XIV and XV Battaglione Coloniale and armoured car units. This group reaches Tug Argan on 10 August.

7. Colonna De Simone attacks Tug Argan on 12 August, deploying II Brigata on the left, which attempts to outflank the enemy by attacking 3/15th Punjab's positions while, in the centre, XIII, XIV and XV Brigata Coloniale attack the positions held by 1st Northern Rhodesia Regiment and 2nd King's Rifles Regiment. To the right, Colonna Bertello approaches the Tug Argan positions. After facing strong resistance, the Italians renew their attack, though still experience no success until 15 August, when General Godwin-Austen orders to withdraw.

16–19 August

8. Facing the withdrawal of enemy forces, the Italians regroup, bringing forward LXX Brigata, Colonna Bertello and the three Battaglione Coloniale. This enables an advance towards Berbera, though the Italians face artillery fire and counter-attacks from 2nd Black Watch, acting as a rearguard.

9. On the evening of 19 August, shortly after the British evacuation from Berbera, Colonna De Simone enters the town, completing the Italian seizure of British Somaliland. The British evacuation takes 5,690 troops, plus a good deal of equipment and weapons, to Aden.

THE ITALIAN CONQUEST OF BRITISH SOMALILAND, 4–19 AUGUST 1940

The conquest of British Somaliland was Italy's only success achieved during the entire war. The aim was to eliminate the British threat to the rear of the Italian positions in Ethiopia and to shorten the line of defence. The operation was planned in July and was to take place alongside Field Marshal Graziani's offensive in Egypt. Graziani's postponements led to this operation taking place first. The plan was based on a three-prong offensive into the arid and deserted area, largely supported by most of the available tanks in East Africa. The attack, which faced no enemy opposition at the start, soon ground to a halt both because of the terrain and the enemy's stubborn resistance at the Tug Argan Pass. Eventually, the British decision to evacuate from Berbera puts an end to the offensive. Seven months later, the South Africans landed at Berbera, putting an end to the Italian occupation of British Somaliland.

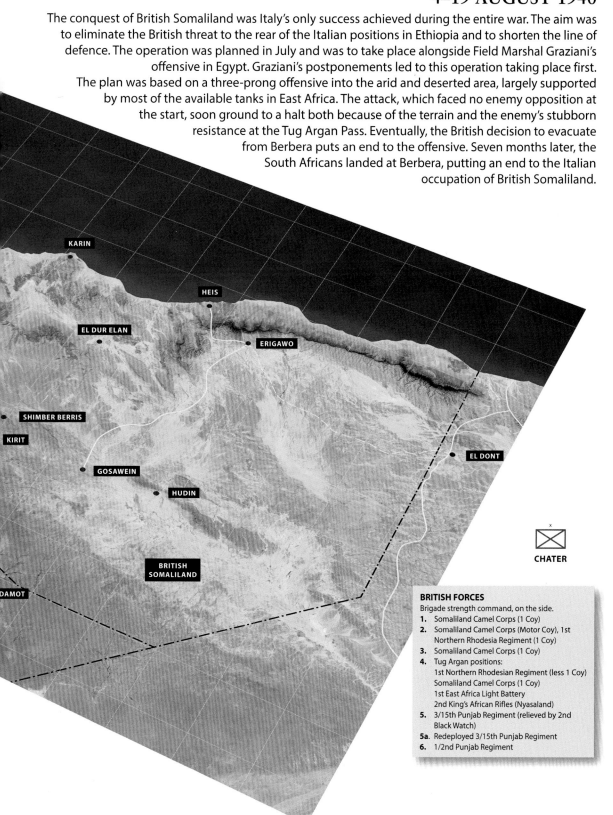

CHATER

BRITISH FORCES
Brigade strength command, on the side.
1. Somaliland Camel Corps (1 Coy)
2. Somaliland Camel Corps (Motor Coy), 1st Northern Rhodesia Regiment (1 Coy)
3. Somaliland Camel Corps (1 Coy)
4. Tug Argan positions:
   1st Northern Rhodesian Regiment (less 1 Coy)
   Somaliland Camel Corps (1 Coy)
   1st East Africa Light Battery
   2nd King's African Rifles (Nyasaland)
5. 3/15th Punjab Regiment (relieved by 2nd Black Watch)
5a. Redeployed 3/15th Punjab Regiment
6. 1/2nd Punjab Regiment

Italian troops advancing in British Somaliland. In the centre is a soldier carrying on his shoulders the spare parts box for the Breda light machine gun, with a heavy machine gun being carried by another soldier on the right. (Photo by ullstein bild via Getty Images)

Argan, which was defended along the main road by the 1st Northern Rhodesia Regiment deployed along the Argan's sandy river bed, with the 2nd KAR also deployed on the hills to the south, while three companies of the 3/15th Punjab defended the northern approaches. The Italians attacked along the main road with the XIV and XV Brigata Coloniale, supported by the XIII Brigata and tanks. The III Brigata from the Colonna di Destra was to attack the positions on the Assa Hills in order to cross the Jerato Pass. Even though the British defences were thinly spread over a wide area, they managed to deal effectively with the Italian forces, which suffered from inadequate logistics. By the 13th, the Italian attack had stalled, in spite of some local successes at Tug Argan and the Assa Hills. However, the Italian superiority in artillery clearly made it impossible to hold the positions indefinitely, and therefore Godwin-Austen informed General Wilson (temporarily replacing Wavell) on 14 August of his decision to start the evacuation if a local counter-attack failed to regain the positions lost. When this duly happened, on the 15th, Wilson ordered the start of the evacuation, which was protected by the rearguard action of the 2nd Black Watch and was completed by 1400hrs on the 18th. Italian troops entered Berbera on the next day.

The short-lived campaign had shown all the weaknesses of the Italian forces, which lost 2,019 men (1,868 colonial) while capturing 64 enemy soldiers along with five field guns, 30 heavy machine guns and 128 motor vehicles. British losses amounted to a total of 260 men, mostly in the

Setting up of the victory flag at a captured British position in the Gulf of Aden, August 1940. (Photo by ullstein bild via Getty Images)

Italian troops inspecting an occupied military position in Sudan in late summer 1940. (Photo by ullstein bild via Getty Images)

Northern Rhodesia Regiment, and even though the loss of Somaliland had its repercussions, it proved that British forces were even capable of outfighting the Italians when inferior in numbers and armament. The Italian seizure of British Somaliland effectively marked the end of the first phase of the East Africa campaign.

THE FIRST STAGE OF THE BRITISH OFFENSIVE

The end of the rainy season was followed by Italian defensive preparations and an almost complete stagnation of operations. Starting from September 1940, the Italians noticed a progressive increase of enemy forces at the borders, particularly in Kenya, and a surge in the domestic insurgency. This led to a reorganization of the area commands, with the Goggiam region being transferred from Scacchiere Nord to Scacchiere Est under the command of General Nasi, who was deemed the best suited to deal with insurgency. The reorganization, completed on 4 February 1941, saw Scacchiere Nord being reduced to defend northern Eritrea (the Massawa, Asmara and Adua areas), while Scacchiere Est took over an area ranging from Amba Alagi in the west to Uebi Scebeli in the south, including the whole of British Somaliland. This enabled Scacchiere Nord to defend the border along with the newly created Scacchiere Ovest (General Nasi was replaced in command of Scacchiere Est by his deputy, Lieutenant-General Sisto Bertoldi) in the Gondar–Dessie–Addis Ababa area. Scacchiere Sud was joined by the newly created Scacchiere Giuba (Juba), formerly the Settore Giuba, to face Kenya. Activity was limited to a series of rather unsuccessful *coups de main* in the Blue Nile area by mid-October, as Amedeo d'Aosta was focused on resisting facing the unavoidable enemy offensive as long as possible. The defences were organized to last as long as possible and, whatever the outcome, Italian forces were to withdraw to a series of redoubts, which included the Massawa–Keren–Asmara area, Dessie, Addis Ababa (surrounded by five other redoubts), the three redoubts at Diredawa, Harar and Jijiga, Mogadishu and two redoubts in the Lake region, along with three others in the area facing southern Sudan. It was, in practice, a complete surrender of the initiative.

THE BATTLE OF TUG ARGAN, 12 AUGUST 1940 (PP.40–41)

The Italian invasion of British Somaliland in August 1940 represented a unique achievement, as this was the only country Italy actually seized during the war. The Italian attack focused on the main road leading from Jijiga to Berbera, which had the Tug Argan Pass, near Haleya, as its main obstacle. The attack, led by General De Simone's central column, was supported by medium tanks of the 322 Compagnia Carri M (medium tanks company). It was made up of 30 M11/39 medium tanks (1) produced in 1939, the first Italian medium tanks to be built. Only 100 M11/39s were built, 30 being sent to East Africa and the remaining 70 to North Africa. The column, mostly composed of colonial units, also included small elements of Italian troops from the 'Granatieri di Savoia' Division (2) and a machine-gun battalion supporting the tanks with heavy Breda 37 and light Breda 30 machine guns (3). It

was joined by the right column commanded by General Bertello, which switched from its main axis of advance towards Burao in order to support the attack on Tug Argan. The Tug Argan position, held by the 1st Northern Rhodesia Regiment and 2nd King's Rifle Regiment, resisted the first Italian attack and managed to repulse the second one until 15 August. The Italians never broke through at Tug Argan, which was abandoned on 15 August upon orders from General Godwin-Austen to withdraw to Berbera to cover the British evacuation from British Somaliland. In all, the Italians deployed three battalions plus 23 colonial ones, along with 21 artillery batteries, supported by medium and light tanks and armoured cars, for a total of 4,800 Italian and some 30,000 colonial troops.

This made the situation easier for General Wavell, who also had his own issues to deal with. With three divisions in Kenya by October 1940 (1st South African and 11th and 12th African), Wavell had at his disposal a force which he deemed not suitable for operations in North Africa, both because of its composition and the different climatic conditions, while Whitehall pressed him to employ there those apparently idle forces. In deciding about operations in East Africa, Wavell had to take into account the growing nervousness in Kenya, Rhodesia and South Africa of a possible Italian invasion. The

Soldiers of the Sudan Defence Force attached to an Indian infantry brigade patrolling the border with Eritrea on 16 December 1940. (Photo by Mirrorpix/Mirrorpix via Getty Images)

first step towards the development of an offensive plan against Italian East Africa was to appoint General Cunningham to command of East Africa on 1 November 1940, followed by a meeting on 2 December in Cairo, during which the overall plan was outlined. In Wavell's view, the steps to be taken were to start with minor operations aimed at the recapture of Kassala while maintaining pressure on Gallabat and increasing the guerrilla activity in East Africa. Subsequently, General Cunningham was to maintain pressure in the Moyale area while preparing for an advance towards Kismayu, which Cunningham deemed not possible until after June 1941, contrary to what Wavell hoped. Wavell's general aim was to secure the area and focus on rebellion, with the intent of withdrawing as many forces as possible in order to reinforce North Africa, where the offensive against the Italian forces in Egypt was just about to start.

Wavell's idea for an offensive against East Africa focused on the northern area, the ideal lines of advance being either Djibouti to Addis Ababa, which had to be ruled out following the Italian invasion of British Somaliland, or from Kassala to Asmara, which was to pave the way for an advance into Eritrea while other forces attacked in the centre against Ethiopia and in the south against Italian Somaliland. The key to the entire campaign was provided by the success of General O'Connor's offensive against Sidi Barrani in Egypt, which enabled Wavell to withdraw the 4th Indian Division (literally taken from the battlefield) and start preparations. These were moved forward, with Wavell ordering the offensive to start on 9 February rather than in March as envisaged. Meanwhile, plans for the insurgency developed into a separate campaign to bring Emperor Haile Selassie back to the throne while a small force, the 'Gazelle Force', started harassing the Italian positions. The seizure of Gallabat and the eventual Italian withdrawal from Kassala gave the signal that Wavell's plan had more than a chance for success, pushing him to focus on a large-scale offensive aimed at collapsing the entire Italian position in East Africa. While the Italian defeat in North Africa supported this aim, the Cabinet's decision in February to send troops to support Greece in view of the forthcoming German offensive created a crisis for Wavell. Rather than halting operations against East Africa in order to focus on the Mediterranean, he ordered them to be continued, warning that forces could have been withdrawn earlier than anticipated. This made the first stage of the British offensive against Italian East Africa decisive, the key to the entire campaign being at Keren.

Dominion and empire forces help mules of the Royal Indian Army Service Corps to negotiate rocky terrain in East Africa on 16 November 1940. (Photo by Lt E.G. Malindine/ Imperial War Museums via Getty Images)

The arrival of the 5th Indian Division enabled plans for the attack against Gallabat, which the Italians had turned into a fortified position. The leading assault force was provided by the 10th Indian Brigade, supported by the Sudan Defence Force (SDF) and eight Matilda tanks from the 6th Royal Tank Regiment. Albeit lacking experience, the men of 10th Brigade managed to infiltrate the Italian positions, which were attacked from the air on 6 November, before an artillery bombardment started and the tanks moved on towards the enemy positions. The Italians (mostly two companies from the 'Granatieri' Division and the IV Brigata Coloniale) stubbornly resisted the assault and the colonial troops even counter-attacked, but the Italians eventually broke and withdrew to Metemma behind the border. Facing the possibility of a strong Italian counter-attack, the British forces, under the command of Brigadier William Slim, eventually withdrew, the entire operation bringing remarkable strategic advantages since the Italians deployed considerable forces in the Gallabat and Metemma garrisons, to the detriment of other areas. At this point, Wavell designed his three-pronged attack plan against Italian East Africa, which was to start with an advance from Sudan in February, followed by an increase in the domestic insurgency in the west, which would enable General Cunningham to attack from Kenya. The offensive was preceded on 16 December by a large-scale raid against El Wak, a frontier post in Kenya about halfway between Moyale and Bardera. Carried out by the 1st South African Brigade, the raid was a complete success, leading to the practical destruction of the Italian defences (CIII Gruppo Dubat, CXCI Battaglione Coloniale) and, above all, achieving complete surprise over the Italian command. This was probably the most important achievement, as the British forces were now fully aware that, in spite of their numerical inferiority, they could rely on speed and movement on unsuitable terrain. This enabled them to attack the isolated Italian garrisons and crumble the entire defences in one area. Psychologically, the offensive would be helped by the fact that the Italians were suffering from their setback in Greece, which, along with high-level intelligence, suggested they might be inclined to surrender.

THE ATTACK FROM SUDAN

Facing the imminent British offensive at the beginning of 1941, Amedeo d'Aosta, acting upon input provided by the commander of Scacchiere Nord, General Frusci, authorized a withdrawal from positions along the border to the defence line inside Eritrea, built along the string of forts running from Cub Cub to Keren, Agordat and Barentu. Only rearguard forces were left at the border – the plan was to preserve available units as much as possible from any fighting against mechanized forces in the unfavourable lowland terrain. At the same time, Scacchiere Nord was reinforced with four Brigate Coloniali taken from the main reserve, which were deployed in Eritrea, while two other brigades (along with other units) were deployed in the Gallabat area. This left Amedeo d'Aosta with two brigades in the Harar area, the 'Granatieri di Savoia' Division, which, along with four battalions from the 'Cacciatori d'Africa' Division, was deployed in the Addis Ababa area, and seven Blackshirts battalions. The overall Italian deployment at the beginning of the offensive saw some 122,000 men in Eritrea and another 122,000 deployed between the Amhara region and British Somaliland. Some 10,000 men were in the area of Addis Ababa, and 55,000 others in south-western Ethiopia (in the Galla-Sidamo Governance), facing southern Sudan and Kenya. A further 27,000 men were deployed in Italian Somaliland, facing Kenya. The Italians greatly overestimated their enemy's capabilities, assuming that the overall British forces amounted to some 210,000–230,000 men, almost equally divided between north and south (100,000 men in Sudan and another 100,000-plus in Kenya). There was also believed to be an additional 5,000 irregulars ready to move from the west and a further 10,000–20,000 men at Aden available to land either in Somaliland or even at Djibouti.

The key to the British offensive in the north was once again Kassala, deemed the only starting position for an advance aimed at the seizure of Asmara and then onto the harbour at Massawa, some 250km away, which would drive the Italians clean out of Eritrea. The newly promoted Lieutenant-General William Platt also had to face difficult terrain, which made supplies hard to maintain, and many troops who lacked experience and knowledge of the terrain. Considering that Platt was aware of the nature and extent of the fortifications in Frusci's Scacchiere Nord area, there was no underestimation of the Italian strength and capabilities. He was also aware that with a ship having been intercepted and detained in the Red Sea, the Italians had not been supplied with anti-tank guns. Furthermore, thanks to the inept Italian intelligence service, Platt was able to deceive them as to his intentions, both by making his own forces appear stronger than they actually were and by creating a series of deceptions aimed at diverting enemy forces. These included the creation of dummy camps suggesting a possible attack along the coast from south of Port Sudan, along with a raid by 'Gazelle Force' against Gallabat, which, even though largely unsuccessful, made the Italians extremely nervous. The attack was made possible by the arrival in December 1940 of 4th Indian Division's 7th Indian Brigade, along with Matilda tanks from the 4th Royal Tank Regiment, which joined the 5th Indian Division. Scheduled to start on 8 February 1941, the operation was moved forward as soon as it became clear that the Italians were actually withdrawing from their positions along the frontier. A new date was set for 18 January, when the 4th Indian Division could not be fully deployed as it was still in the process of moving

A soldier from a camel patrol of the Sudan Defence Force attached to the 9th Indian Infantry Brigade uses his camel to aim his rifle on the Eritrean frontier in 1940. (Photo by No. 1 Army Film and Photo Section, AFPU/Imperial War Museums via Getty Images)

The advance in the north, 18 January–8 April 1941

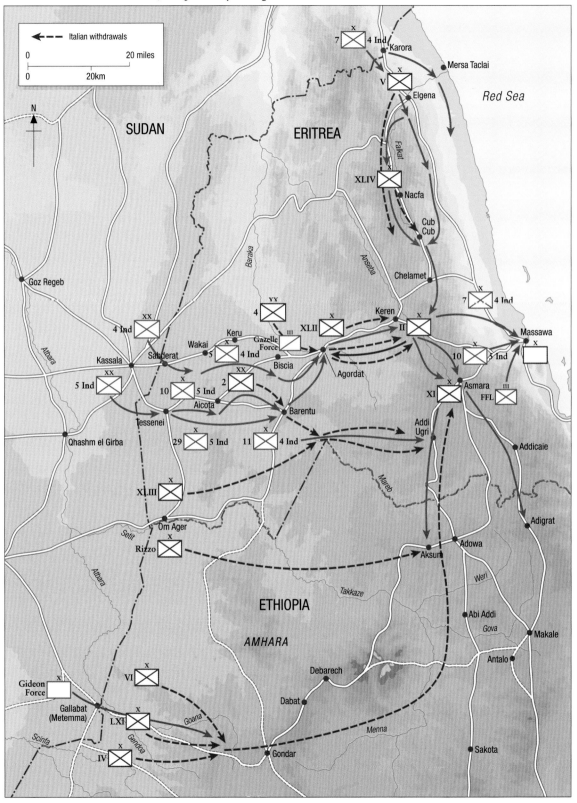

from Egypt. By then, HQ Troops Sudan had at its disposal the 7th Indian Brigade on the coastal sector, Northern Force (made up of HQ 4th Indian Division, 'Gazelle Force' and 11th Indian Brigade) in the Kassala area and Southern Force (comprising HQ 5th Indian Division and 9th, 10th and 29th Indian Brigades) in the Gedaref area, to the north-east of Gallabat.

Their flanks protected by 'Gazelle Force', the leading elements of 4th Indian Division entered Kassala on 19 January, only to find it abandoned by the Italians. Uncertain as to the extent of the Italian withdrawal, Platt's forces were split to head in different directions. The 4th Indian Division advanced into Eritrea, following the path to the east, past Sabderat in the direction of Keru. The 5th Indian Division moved to the south, following the road to Tessenei, from there moving along the main road flanking the Mareb River to Aicota. To the north, 'Gazelle Force', preceding 11th Indian Brigade, led the advance, encountering an Italian position at Wakai, some 20km east of Kassala, on the 19th. However, before the position could be attacked the next day, the Italians withdrew, 'Gazelle Force' resuming its pursuit. The first resistance was met on 21 January at Keru, east of Kassala, just as the 5th Indian Division (now led by the 10th Indian Brigade) reached Aicota and detached a mechanized column formed around the 2nd Motor Machine Gun Group to the north, trying to outflank the Italian positions at Keru. 5th Indian Division's advance was now slowed down by Italian resistance, the mechanized column being halted by an Italian infantry battalion south of Keru for one day. The rest of the division, advancing in the direction of Barentu with 29th Brigade, was also slowed down by terrain and Italian resistance.

Keru, a naturally strong position held by five battalions from the Italian XLI Brigata Coloniale, was the location of the first battle fought in this new phase of the East Africa campaign. The Italians reacted to the approach of 'Gazelle Force' by launching a cavalry charge, which was halted just some 20m before they reached the field gun positions. This was followed by another attack, this time by infantry, which was also repulsed. On 22 January, 4th Sikhs attacked and seized a position south of Keru, which was then assaulted and found to be strongly defended. As 4th Sikhs were fighting hard at Keru, 11th Brigade reached them with 2nd Camerons joining the attack, while the rest of the brigade attempted to outflank the Italian positions but without success. This was actually achieved by 10th Brigade, which, advancing from the south, reached Bahar to the east of Keru, cutting off the Italian forces, whose remnants withdrew at night. They eventually clashed with 10th Brigade during the withdrawal, suffering heavy casualties. The success could not be exploited at once, however, since 'Gazelle Force' was held up and could not resume its advance until 25 January, when its leading elements approached Agordat, cutting off the road to Barentu. On the next day, the bulk of 5th Brigade, supported by B Squadron of the 4th Royal Tank Regiment reached Biscia, about halfway to Agordat, which 'Gazelle Force' discovered could not be outflanked by mechanized troops. This made Agordat, defended by three colonial brigades (II, XII and XLII) and three Blackshirts battalions, supported by artillery and a German motorized company, the key to the Italian defence in the area. The leading unit, 4th Sikhs, made contact with the Italian forces at Agordat in the afternoon of 27 January; the next day, two brigades (5th Indian on the left and 11th Indian on the right) moved on to and attacked Agordat. The following day,

A line-up of Italian M11/39 medium tanks captured at Agordat in February 1941. (British Army, public domain, via Wikimedia Commons)

the 29th, the attackers were halted by strong Italian defences, which compelled them to withdraw and reorganize. Another attack on the night of 29 January was more successful, even though it was stopped once again by Italian defences focused on the dominating Mount Cochen. Here, the Italians managed to bring forward some guns that compelled the Indians to reorganize and withdraw, leaving only two companies of 1st Rajputanas on top of the hill. On 31 January, 5th Brigade attacked the main Italian position at Agordat, seizing most of it. The supporting tanks advanced along the road to Keren, meeting Italian tanks preparing a counter-attack. Their destruction opened the road to Keren and the Italians hastily withdrew. The Italian forces defending Barentu also launched their last counter-attack, but following its failure, they started a withdrawal, leaving only rearguards behind. With Barentu seized on 2 February, 'Gazelle Force' approached the area of Keren.

While the 4th and 5th Indian Divisions opened the way to Keren, 9th Indian Brigade contained the Italian forces near Gallabat while a railroad was being built to connect Kassala to Tessenei. Already in early January 1941, British intelligence reckoned that the Italians intended to withdraw from Gallabat, the first sign of such a move being noticed on 30 January. 9th Indian Brigade was then instructed to pursue the Italians with a mechanized column, which started its advance following the actual Italian withdrawal on the night of 31 January/1 February. It soon became clear that the Italians were withdrawing here in a more organized and methodical way, mining the road and relying on thick undergrowth to prevent outflanking movements. Mine clearing became the main issue of the Indian advance until, on 10 February, contact was made with Arbegnoch forces at Wahni. Having reached a position about halfway between Gallabat and Gondar, the Indian forces halted, 9th Brigade starting to regroup at Gedaref in Sudan. The decisive battle was now to be fought at Keren.

THE FIRST BATTLE OF KEREN

General Frusci's reaction to the British offensive had been largely successful, as the Italians managed to pull back the bulk of their border forces (1st, 4th and 2nd Divisione Coloniale, with a total of six colonial brigades and seven independent ones) to the Keren plateau without suffering heavy losses and in spite of their many difficulties. These included an almost complete breakdown in communication, due to non-functioning radio sets, and the struggle in supplying troops in the difficult terrain, which required the use of airdrops. The most important consequence of Platt's offensive was the reorganization of the Italian commands, with Frusci now in charge of Eritrea alone, while the newly formed Scacchiere Ovest took over in the Amhara and Gojjam regions. In the first days of February, the remnants of the II, XLII and

XII Brigata Coloniale withdrew to Keren, along with the artillery from Agordat, losing a great deal of equipment in the process, including almost all their motor vehicles, which had to be destroyed. The Italian forces lost 179 officers, 130 NCOs, 1,230 Italian other ranks and 14,686 African other ranks. Ninety-six field guns were also lost, along with 141 motor vehicles, 15 light and nine medium tanks. The XII Brigata was then used to form the 3 Divisione, deployed between Keren and Arresa to block the Keren–Asmara road, but during the last ten days of January, the Italian withdrawal turned into a rout, which, along with the lack of a clear vision amongst the superior commanders, would influence the defence of Keren.

Men from a Scottish regiment marching through the town of Asmara, an important centre of communications, on the Allies' victorious advance into Eritrea on 1 April 1941. (Photo by Mirrorpix/Mirrorpix via Getty Images)

At the top of the plateau, Keren presented one of the most formidable natural defences that had to be overcome during the whole of World War II. The main road from Agordat climbed through a gradually narrowing gorge before rising for several thousand metres to reach Keren, which, although lacking modern fortifications (the forts were nothing more than a series of trenches protected by walls made from mud), was protected by a series of peaks. To the north-west of the road were Brig's Peak and Mount Sanchil, and to the front was Cameron Ridge, steep peaks covered with boulders and scrubs and razor-edge ridges. Fort Dologorodoc, to the east, provided an equally commanding feature, along with Mount Zeban and Mount Falestoh, all making any attack difficult and surely costly. Since the defences of Keren were not manned in early February, 11 Reggimento 'Granatieri di Savoia' (11th Infantry Regiment) under Colonel Corsi was diverted to take up positions in the area, followed by the XI Brigata Coloniale and the III Gruppo Squadroni Cavalleria Coloniale, IV Gruppo Cavalleria Coloniale,

Battle of Keren, 1 February 1941

BRITISH
4th Indian Infantry Division – Major-General Noel Beresford-Peirse
11th Indian Infantry Brigade, Brigadier Reginald Savory (2nd Queen's Own Cameron Highlanders, 1/6th [Wellesley's] Rajputana Rifles, 3/1st Punjab Regiment, 3/14th Punjab Regiment)
51st (Middle East) Commando
Gazelle Force

ITALIAN
Scacchiere Nord – Lieutenant-General Luigi Frusci
1 Divisione Coloniale, General Nicola Carminio
11 Reggimento 'Granatieri di Savoia' (Colonnello Corsi), with I (Granatieri), II (Granatieri), III (Bersaglieri)
Battaglione Alpini 'Uork Ambra', I Battaglione Mitraglieri from

10 Reggimento Granatieri
XI Brigata Coloniale (Colonnello Prina), with: LI, LII, LVI, LXIII battaglione coloniale
III Gruppo Squadroni Cavalleria Coloniale
IV Gruppo Squadroni Cavalleria Coloniale
CIV Gruppo Artiglieria 77/28
CVI Gruppo Artiglieria autoportato
Elements from 4 Divisione Coloniale (remnants, the division being disbanded)

Divisional elements joining the battle:
II Brigata Coloniale
V Brigata Coloniale
XLII Brigata Coloniale
V Gruppo Artiglieria

Indian Army soldiers with an armoured car on the front line at the battle of Keren in Eritrea in April 1941. (Photo by Mirrorpix via Getty Images)

CIV Gruppo Artiglieria and elements of the 4 Divisione Coloniale withdrawing from Agordat. These forces, although not excessively strong and lacking artillery, proved enough to halt Platt's advance during the first battle of Keren.

On 1 February, the 5th Brigade seized Agordat, taking 300 prisoners, before advancing towards Keren, 'Gazelle Force's' pursuit of the withdrawing Italians having been halted by a blown bridge. Its subsequent advance was also held up by a well-defended Italian roadblock, while 11th Brigade took up positions close to Keren. Immediately after a field reconnaissance, the commander of 11th Brigade drew up an attack plan which envisaged the 2nd Camerons capturing the spur leading to Cameron Ridge while 1st Rajputanas seized a gap south of Mount Scialaco, which soon proved to be impassable. Although 2nd Camerons was able to seize its target without opposition, it struggled on almost impassable terrain. As 1st Rajputanas was unable to execute the original flank attack, the plan was changed to focus on the attempt to seize Brig's Peak and Mount Sanchil, dominant features overlooking the Dongolas Gorge and the road leading to Keren. While the area was reconnoitred, 2nd Camerons consolidated its position, eventually capturing the top of Cameron Ridge, just before Mount Sanchil. With the 3/14th Punjab detached for the task, the attack started at 1930hrs on 4 February with 2nd Camerons' attempt to reach the top of Brig's Peak, only to be forced to withdraw by the Italian defenders. The 3/14th Punjab attacked and seized Brig's Peak at 2300hrs on the 4th, the area (consisting of three peaks) being fully secured by 0345hrs the next morning. This enabled an attack on nearby Mount Sanchil at 0700hrs on 5 February, with part of the mountain seized within 90 minutes, but with troops there facing Italian artillery and machine guns. As its observation officers were either killed or wounded, 3/14th Punjab no longer had any contact with their artillery forces and therefore could provide no support.

Facing heavy casualties and an ammunition shortage, along with the impossibility of bringing reinforcements from Cameron Ridge, 3/14th Punjab was unable to resist the Italian counter-attacks and some of its units started withdrawing. Reports of the withdrawal came shortly after 1st Rajputanas and 2nd Camerons had been ordered to provide support to 3/14th Punjab, which led to new instructions: the units were to hold the high ground to the west of Brig's Peak and Mount Sanchil while also attempting to hold Mount Sanchil. At 1345hrs, an Italian counter-attack reached the top of Brig's Peak. Even though it was repulsed, this led to the decision to abandon the position, which the 3/14th Punjab did after suffering the loss of 116 men. Nightfall on 5 February saw 2nd Camerons and 1st Rajputanas in position at Cameron Ridge, with 3/14th Punjab collected at the bottom of the hill and 3/1st Punjab ready to approach. The two forward battalions were attacked five separate times by the Italians on 6 February, all assaults being easily repulsed. To prevent a possible outflanking movement, 'Gazelle Force' seized Mount Tafala and Mount Jepio to the west of Cameron Ridge. Another Italian counter-attack at 1200hrs was also repulsed, with heavy losses on both sides. The same happened with a counter-attack that lasted from 1530–1730hrs, during which 3/1st Punjab moved in support of 1st Rajputanas. Two hours later, the Italians counter-attacked again, a final assault coming at 2330hrs, both being repulsed.

Despite the struggles to break through to Keren, Platt knew it was a key area and refused to reconsider his options. The area had to be seized before the onset of the rainy season, otherwise it would be impossible to advance any further due to the climate and terrain. Thus, on 6 February, as the Italians counter-attacked, 5th Indian Brigade was prepared for a further assault while seeking alternatives. Relying on Italian low morale, an attempt was made at the Acqua Gap, to the east of the road to Keren. The position, dominated by Mount Falestoh and Mount Zelale, was formidable but was defended by only two colonial battalions deemed to have suffered from desertion. The attack was carried out by 5th Brigade, supported by 11th Brigade, which was to distract the Italians while 5th Brigade advanced through the 'happy valley' to reach the Acqua Gap. The attack, starting on 7 February, saw the leading battalions coming under heavy mortar and machine-gun fire and soon dispersing, while the attempt to seize the Acqua Gap and the dominating feature to its west encountered stiff resistance. Even though both were eventually taken, an Italian counter-attack drove the two companies away, leaving Rajputana Ridge to the south as the only position 5th Brigade could take. With the surprise attack having failed, there was no other choice than withdrawal, 5th Brigade being replaced at Acqua Gap by 'Gazelle Force' on the night of 9/10 February. On 8 February, the Italian forces at Keren were reinforced by Alpini

An Indian motorized column advancing towards Keren. The area, as can be seen, offered a natural defensive position which the Italians fully exploited. (Australian War Memorial, 007082)

Indian troops in a trench in a position overlooking Mount Sanchil, Keren, in March 1941. (Australian Official Photographer, public domain, via Wikimedia Commons)

Battalion 'Uork Ambra' from 10 Reggimento Granatieri and XLIV Brigata Coloniale, bringing about a few changes in the Italian deployment. The Mount Falestoh area was now defended by II Brigata Coloniale and I Battaglione Granatieri, with the Mount Dologorodoc–Mount Sanchil area held by III Battaglione Bersaglieri, with three colonial battalions in reserve. The 'Uork Ambra' Battalion deployed at Mount Agher, while on the 10th, XLIV Brigata was moved away from Keren.

At this point, thanks to the intervention of the 4th Indian Division, a major British attack plan was developed. It consisted of three distinct phases, starting with the seizure of Brig's Peak, followed by the taking of the Acqua Gap and 5th Brigade's advance towards Keren, enabling the entire available force to advance and capture the location. The attack faced XI Brigata Coloniale at Mount Sanchil, V Brigata Coloniale at Brig's Peak and II Brigata Coloniale to the north-west at Mount Samanna. Mount Zelale and the Acqua Gap were defended by two battalions from II Brigata, while Mount Falestoh was held by II Battalion of 11 Reggimento. The attack started at 1500hrs on 10 February with 11th Brigade seizing the Brig's Peak area, though it soon faced an Italian counter-attack, which drove back some units but failed to dislodge the brigade from two positions that were held in the face of yet another attack. Another Italian counter-attack started at 2300hrs on 11 February, leading to infiltration between the two positions the next morning, with the result that the British attack was called off and the units in the Brig's Peak area were withdrawn. At 0300hrs on the 12th, the British attack against the Acqua Gap began, facing stiff Italian resistance and immediate counter-attacks. Since it proved impossible to provide the necessary reinforcements, the attack stalled and was eventually cancelled, British casualties totalling more than 300 men. Both 'Gazelle Force' and 5th Brigade were redeployed on 14 February, effectively bringing to an end the first battle for Keren, which had ended without success.

THE SECOND BATTLE OF KEREN

While the battle for Keren raged, the 7th Indian Infantry Brigade, which had arrived at Port Sudan on 1 January 1941, started its advance along the Red Sea coast, moving towards Keren from the north. The area was defended by V Brigata Coloniale, plus five colonial battalions and one cavalry group, deployed in a series of strongholds along the road leading to Keren. After an initial period of 'aggressive patrolling' on 23–24 January, a first move was made along the road against Karora at the border. However, the attack was called off and 7th Brigade lost the element of surprise. Instead, it was decided to stage a large-scale attack along the coast and the road with the aim of establishing necessary supply bases for further advances. The attack eventually started on 9 February with the seizure of Karora, facing little opposition. On the next day, Mersa Taclai, on the coast, was seized without any opposition at all, while the 1st Royal Sussex seized Elgena on the main road. Even though the advance had not solved the logistical problems, it continued with two ad hoc columns formed by the 1st Royal Sussex: Meadowforce, mounted on camels, advancing towards Nacfa, and the motorized Cubcol, moving towards Cub Cub. Contact was made with the withdrawing Italian units on 14 February, just before 7th Brigade's headquarters was requested to exercise pressure on Keren from the north. With the 4th Machine Gun Company now in the lead, 7th Brigade reached Cub Cub by 22 February, with the leading elements of Cubcol reaching Chelamet,

Indian troops standing next to a signpost for the city of Keren (Cheren) after its seizure on 27 March 1941. (Australian War Memorial, 007080)

to the north of Keren, on 23 and 24 February. The next step was to reach the Meschelit Pass, which, with a series of turns, led to Keren some 30km to the south. The supply situation could only be solved with extensive works, which required time, so 7th Brigade carried on as is. It reached the Meschelit Pass to find it heavily defended by the Italians. However, 7th Brigade managed to capture it on 28 February without any loss. The advance was resumed on 3 March and the 1st Royal Sussex reached Mendad, some 10km north of Keren, while the 4th Machine Gun Company advanced along the coast. Finding the terrain difficult and facing the Italian defences to the north of Keren, 7th Brigade basically halted its advance, relying on the fact that it had distracted a number of Italian forces from the defence of Keren, which was

---

Battle of Keren, 13 March 1941

BRITISH
British Troops in the Sudan – Lieutenant General William Platt
4th Indian Division, Major-General Noel Beresford-Peirse
11th Indian Infantry Brigade
(2nd Camerons Highlanders, 1/6th Rajputana Rifles, 2/5th Mahratta Light Infantry, 1st Royal Fusiliers, [attached from 5th Brigade] 4/6th Rajputana Rifles [attached from 5th Brigade])
5th Indian Infantry Brigade
(3/1st Punjab Regiment, 4/11th Sikh Regiment [attached from 7th Brigade], A and B Squadron Central India Horse)
10th Indian Infantry Brigade (attached)
(4/10th Baluch Regiment, 3/18th Royal Garhwal Rifles)
5th Indian Division, Major-General Lewis Heat
9th Indian Infantry Brigade
(2nd West Yorkshire, 3/5th Mahratta Light Infantry, 3/12th Royal Frontier Force Regiment, 2nd Highland Light Infantry [attached from 10th Brigade])
29th Indian Infantry Brigade
(1st Worcestershire Regiment, 3/2nd Punjab Regiment, 6th Royal/13th Frontier Force Rifles)
7th Indian Infantry Brigade
(1st Royal Sussex, 4/16th Punjab Regiment)

Briggs Force, Brigadier Harold Briggs
Brigade d'orient (French Foreign Legion), (1er Bataillon Legion Etrangere, Bataillon de Marche 3)

ITALIAN
Scacchiere Nord – Lieutenant-General Luigi Frusci
11th Reggimento 'Granatieri di Savoia' (I-II Granatieri, III Bersaglieri)
Battaglione Alpini 'Uork Ambra'
11 Legione CCNN
Battaglione CCNN XI, XLIV
II Brigata Coloniale (V, IX, X, CLI)
V Brigata Coloniale (XCVII, CVI)
VI Brigata Coloniale (XIX, XXIV, XXXI, XXXIV)
XI Brigata Coloniale (under command at various times: XIII, L, LI, LII, LV, LVI, LVII, LXII)
XII Brigata Coloniale (XXXVI, XLI, CIII)
XLIV Brigata Coloniale (CV, CVII)
Battaglione Coloniale 'Tipo', XXXVI, L, LVIII, LXIII, LXX, CXXXI, CXXXII, IC
XV Gruppo Squadroni Cavalleria
Gruppo Artiglieria II, V, VI, XI, XII, XLIV

THE ASSAULT AT KEREN, 16 MARCH 1941 (PP.54–55)

The battle of Keren was the turning point of the entire East Africa campaign. The Italian positions at Keren were attacked for the first time by 4th Indian Division in February 1941, the assaults being repulsed thanks to superior forces and the defences built on impregnable hills. In order to break through the Italian positions, both the 4th and 5th Indian Infantry Divisions were deployed, their second attack starting on 15 March after several days of artillery bombing of the Italian positions. The initial plan was to see the 4th Indian Division attacking to the north and east of the main road leading to Keren, while the 5th Division attacked to the south and east. The latter **(1)**, advancing on the Dongolas Gorge, stormed and seized the key position of Fort Dologorodoc on 16 March, marking a decisive moment in the battle. The fort, in fact nothing more than a series of mud walls and trenches built to protect the height, was defended by colonial units and the elite Alpini (mountain infantry) Battalion 'Uork Ambra' **(2)**, which failed to regain control of the fort in spite of repeated attempts made with several counter-attacks **(3)**. The seizure of Fort Dologorodoc eventually enabled Matilda tanks to move along the main road and, in spite of a roadblock, advance towards Keren until the Italian positions on the dominating hills collapsed, leading to its seizure on 27 March. The capture of Keren, accelerated by the taking of Massawa on 8 April by 7th Indian Brigade, paved the way for the advance inland, leading the 5th Indian Division to seize Asmara on 1 April and to the subsequent advance to Adowa and Adigrat.

true since they were facing six colonial and one Blackshirts battalion.

On 12 February, Platt had come to the conclusion that the entire strength of both the 4th and 5th Indian Divisions was needed to seize Keren, which led to the disbandment of 'Gazelle Force' and the arrival of 51st Commando as a further reinforcement. The latter unit carried out a series of patrols in the early days of March against the forward Italian defences in order to establish their actual consistency and capabilities. Following their successful defence during the first battle, the Italians had reorganized their forces by creating a series of strongholds to meet any further attacks. XI Brigata Coloniale held the Acqua Gap along with the Battaglione Bersaglieri at Fort Hill, to the south of Fort Dologorodoc. West of the Dongolas Gorge, V and II Brigata Coloniale held a series of hills along with 10 and 11 Reggimento Granatieri, with elements from V and VI Brigata Coloniale holding the Dongolas Gorge area. Both the XII and VI Brigata Coloniale acted as reinforcements, newly arrived at Keren along with 11 Legione Camicie Nere and other units, bringing the total of the defending forces to 21 colonial and seven Italian battalions with a strength of about 12,000 men (17,000 in the British estimate), supported by about 120 guns. This time, Platt focused on a frontal assault, although attempts to outflank the Italian positions were not abandoned, the 1/6th Rajputanas trying to find a way around Mount Scialaco between 4 and 8 February. Reconnaissance to the north was also carried out, but no weak spot could be found in the Italian defences.

An Indian 25-pdr field gun firing against the Italian positions at Keren, March 1941. (Library of Congress, public domain, via Wikimedia Commons)

The attack plan, prepared on 1 March, foresaw both the 4th and 5th Indian Divisions attacking together, the first against Mount Sanchil, Brig's Peak and the area north and west of the Dongolas Gorge, the second moving against the Italian defences to the east of the main road to Keren, focusing on Mount Dologorodoc and Mount Zeban, moving after the former in order to allow maximum artillery support. No definite objectives were set for the first stage, the actual aims to be defined by success on the battleground. 4th Division planned a two-brigade attack, with 11th Brigade moving against the Mount Sanchil area and 5th Brigade attacking Mount Samanna. 5th Division's commander planned a simple attack, 9th Brigade in the lead moving against Falestoh and 29th Brigade advancing against Mount Zeban and the crossroads, with 10th Brigade being kept ready for exploitation. Royal Air Force bombers, having achieved aerial superiority over the area, would provide direct support, bombing the Italian defences during daylight. Troops were deployed on 15 March, Platt conscious that the Italians not only enjoyed the advantage of terrain but were superior in strength.

The attack started at 0700hrs on 15 March, a day marked by extreme hot weather, with an artillery bombardment against the Italian positions at Mount Sanchil and Brig's Peak. The 2nd Mahratta moved against the Italians once the bombardment was finished. 2nd Camerons provided reinforcements, but in spite of repeated attempts, stiff Italian opposition denied the attackers any success and inflicted heavy casualties. While the fighting at Sanchil and Brig's

THE SEIZURE OF KEREN, 13–27 MARCH 1941

Two positions dominated the roads leading from Sudan to Ethiopia: Massawa, on the coast, and Keren, to the west. The battle of Keren, fought between February and March 1941, was the fiercest struggle of the entire campaign and saw the eventual involvement of 4th and 5th Indian Divisions, which was made necessary after the failure of 4th Indian Division in February to break through the Italian defences running along the mountain range to the west of the Keren valley. Once again, this attack clashed with stubborn and determined Italian resistance, which was broken only by a series of frontal attacks in which the Indian infantry climbed steep rocky cliffs and charged the enemy with fixed bayonets. The key feature of Fort Dologorodoc was soon seized, and although troops from Granatieri d'Africa Division led a series of counter-attacks, the road was eventually opened for the Matilda tanks, which entered Keren following the eventual Italian withdrawal.

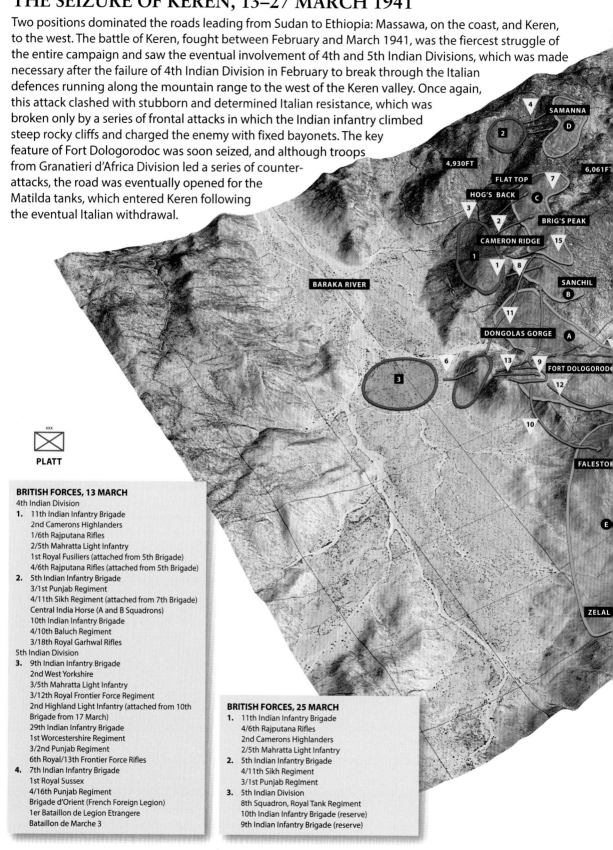

PLATT

BRITISH FORCES, 13 MARCH
4th Indian Division
1. 11th Indian Infantry Brigade
   2nd Camerons Highlanders
   1/6th Rajputana Rifles
   2/5th Mahratta Light Infantry
   1st Royal Fusiliers (attached from 5th Brigade)
   4/6th Rajputana Rifles (attached from 5th Brigade)
2. 5th Indian Infantry Brigade
   3/1st Punjab Regiment
   4/11th Sikh Regiment (attached from 7th Brigade)
   Central India Horse (A and B Squadrons)
   10th Indian Infantry Brigade
   4/10th Baluch Regiment
   3/18th Royal Garhwal Rifles
5th Indian Division
3. 9th Indian Infantry Brigade
   2nd West Yorkshire
   3/5th Mahratta Light Infantry
   3/12th Royal Frontier Force Regiment
   2nd Highland Light Infantry (attached from 10th
   Brigade from 17 March)
   29th Indian Infantry Brigade
   1st Worcestershire Regiment
   3/2nd Punjab Regiment
   6th Royal/13th Frontier Force Rifles
4. 7th Indian Infantry Brigade
   1st Royal Sussex
   4/16th Punjab Regiment
   Brigade d'Orient (French Foreign Legion)
   1er Bataillon de Legion Etrangere
   Bataillon de Marche 3

BRITISH FORCES, 25 MARCH
1. 11th Indian Infantry Brigade
   4/6th Rajputana Rifles
   2nd Camerons Highlanders
   2/5th Mahratta Light Infantry
2. 5th Indian Infantry Brigade
   4/11th Sikh Regiment
   3/1st Punjab Regiment
3. 5th Indian Division
   8th Squadron, Royal Tank Regiment
   10th Indian Infantry Brigade (reserve)
   9th Indian Infantry Brigade (reserve)

SAMANNA
4,930FT
6,061FT
FLAT TOP
HOG'S BACK
BRIG'S PEAK
CAMERON RIDGE
SANCHIL
BARAKA RIVER
DONGOLAS GORGE
FORT DOLOGORODOC
FALESTOH
ZELAL

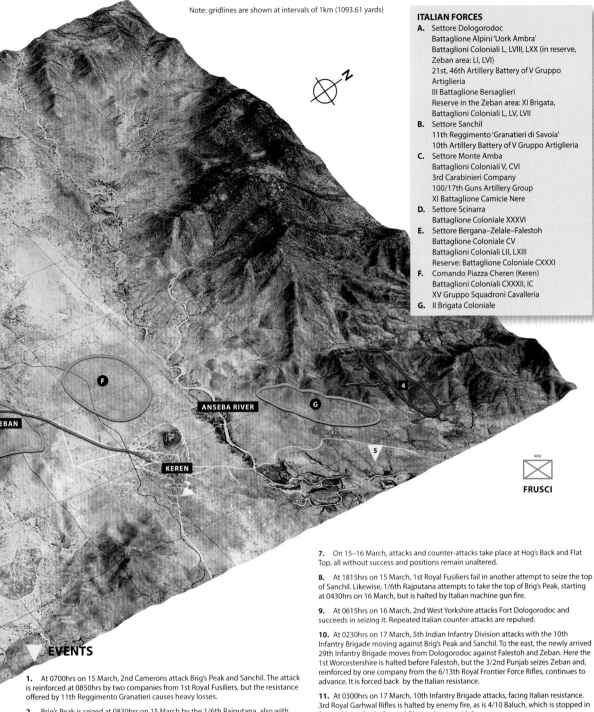

Note: gridlines are shown at intervals of 1km (1093.61 yards)

ITALIAN FORCES

A. Settore Dologorodoc
Battaglione Alpini 'Uork Ambra'
Battaglioni Coloniali L, LVIII, LXX (in reserve, Zeban area: LI, LVI)
21st, 46th Artillery Battery of V Gruppo Artiglieria
III Battaglione Bersaglieri
Reserve in the Zeban area: XI Brigata, Battaglioni Coloniali L, LV, LVII

B. Settore Sanchil
11th Reggimento 'Granatieri di Savoia'
10th Artillery Battery of V Gruppo Artiglieria

C. Settore Monte Amba
Battaglioniaii V, CVI
3rd Carabinieri Company
100/17th Guns Artillery Group
XI Battaglione Camicie Nere

D. Settore Scinarra
Battaglione Coloniale XXXVI

E. Settore Bergana–Zelale–Falestoh
Battaglione Coloniale CV
Battaglioni Coloniali LII, LXIII
Reserve: Battaglione Coloniale CXXXI

F. Comando Piazza Cheren (Keren)
Battaglioni Coloniali CXXXII, IC
XV Gruppo Squadroni Cavalleria

G. II Brigata Coloniale

ANSEBA RIVER

EBAN

KEREN

FRUSCI

EVENTS

1. At 0700hrs on 15 March, 2nd Camerons attack Brig's Peak and Sanchil. The attack is reinforced at 0850hrs by two companies from 1st Royal Fusiliers, but the resistance offered by 11th Reggimento Granatieri causes heavy losses.

2. Brig's Peak is seized at 0830hrs on 15 March by the 1/6th Rajputana, also with heavy losses. Brigadier Savory switches the axis of the attack and redeploys the 11th Brigade. It faces a series of Italian counterattacks that are all repulsed.

3. At 0700hrs on 15 March, 2/5th Mahratta attacks Flat Top, facing barbed wire and artillery fire. Attacks from the flank are unsuccessful but D Company seizes the objective at 1440hrs and is reinforced by the 3rd Royal Garhwal Rifles at 1600hrs. Heavy casualties prevent any further advance.

4. On 15 March, at 0700hrs, 4/11th Sikh advances to and secures Mount Samanna. Strong Italian resistance makes further advance impossible.

5. 1st Royal Sussex, from 7th Indian Brigade, launches a diversionary operation from the north on 13 March after completing its advance. It is joined for the second phase of the attack by the French Brigade d'Orient, but the attack is halted on 15 March.

6. On 15 March, 5th Indian Division attacks the area south of Fort Dologorodoc, with 2nd Highland Light Infantry's advance soon halted by enemy fire. At 1700hrs, a new attack is made by 3/15th Mahratta, which secures the area by 2000hrs, thus enabling 3rd Royal Frontier Force to complete its task by 0005hrs on 16 March. At 0400hrs, the Italian counter-attack is beaten off.

7. On 15–16 March, attacks and counter-attacks take place at Hog's Back and Flat Top, all without success and positions remain unaltered.

8. At 1815hrs on 15 March, 1st Royal Fusiliers fail in another attempt to seize the top of Sanchil. Likewise, 1/6th Rajputana attempts to take the top of Brig's Peak, starting at 0430hrs on 16 March, but is halted by Italian machine gun fire.

9. At 0615hrs on 16 March, 2nd West Yorkshire attacks Fort Dologorodoc and succeeds in seizing it. Repeated Italian counter-attacks are repulsed.

10. At 0230hrs on 17 March, 5th Indian Infantry Division attacks with the 10th Infantry Brigade moving against Brig's Peak and Sanchil. To the east, the newly arrived 29th Infantry Brigade moves from Dologorodoc against Falestoh and Zeban. Here the 1st Worcestershire is halted before Falestoh, but the 3/2nd Punjab seizes Zeban and, reinforced by one company from the 6/13th Royal Frontier Force Rifles, continues to advance. It is forced back by the Italian resistance.

11. At 0300hrs on 17 March, 10th Infantry Brigade attacks, facing Italian resistance. 3rd Royal Garhwal Rifles is halted by enemy fire, as is 4/10 Baluch, which is stopped in front of Brig's Peak. General Platt orders to withdraw.

12. Between 18 and 22 March, the Italians carry out several counter-attacks against enemy-held Fort Dologorodoc and, on the 19th, General Lorenzini is killed during one of these unsuccessful attempts to take back the fort. In the meantime, 9th Infantry Brigade takes over positions at the fort, with 29th Brigade redeployed to the south.

13. At 0430hrs on 25 March, 10th Infantry Brigade attacks along the road to Keren, taking the Italians by surprise. After seizing the objective by 1025hrs, 2nd Field Company clear a way through the road obstruction to enable a further advance at 1430hrs on 26 March by the Matilda tanks of the 8th Squadron RTR.

14. At 0430hrs on 27 March, 3rd Royal Garhwal (under the 29th Brigade) attacks without artillery support, taking the Italians by surprise and seizing Zeban at 0730hrs.

15. At 0600hrs on 27 March, Italian troops at Sanchil surrender. It is seized at 1000hrs.

16. At 0500hrs on 27 March, the Fletcher Force (comprising B Squadron, 4th RTR with eight Matilda tanks plus a carrier troop from Central India Horses with 53 carriers supplied by 9th and 10th Brigade plus 3/1st Punjab) advances towards Keren. It enters Keren soon after the Italian withdrawal.

KEREN · ZEBAN · FALESTOH · ROAD BLOCK · SANCHIL · FORT DOLOGORODOC · PINNACLE · CAMERON RIDGE

THE CLIFFS OF KEREN. "Beyond the plain, a sudden wall of razor ridges, pure rock at the top." The Italians blew down 200 yards of cliff to seal the gorge, and honey-combed the rocks with artillery and machine-gun posts.

A view of the mountains defending the approach to Keren. Cameron Ridge is in the foreground, while on the left are Mount Sanchil and Zeban. To the right are Fort Dologorodoc and Mount Falestoh. (From *The Abyssinian Campaigns: The Official Story of the Conquest of Italian East Africa*, HSMO, published 1942, public domain)

Peak continued, with the defenders successfully holding their positions, 2nd Camerons and 1/6th Rajputanas moved against the Italian positions to the west of Brig's Peak. Here too, heavy casualties were suffered by the attackers, who faced an immediate Italian counter-attack followed by other attacks that lasted through the night. Eventually, 1/6th Rajputanas was able to hold the Hog's Back feature at the centre of the Italian defences, which enabled the 11th Brigade commander to focus in this area with other units. Even though the new attack was not completely successful and the units involved suffered heavy losses, at dusk the brigade still held the positions acquired and prepared for the 1st Royal Fusiliers to move against Mount Sanchil the next day. The attack of 5th Brigade to the west, against Mount Samanna, was greatly helped by artillery support, which prevented the Italians from inflicting casualties. Subsequently, the Italian defences were strengthened and the attackers not only suffered heavy losses – a total of 120 men during the day – but also failed to capture two of the three dominating features of Mount Samanna. Diversionary operations by 7th Brigade were carried out to the north of Keren, but the key to the success was in 5th Division's attacks.

After supporting 4th Indian Division's attack, artillery support switched to the 5th Division's area, and 9th Brigade went on to attack at 1030hrs, with 2nd Highland in the lead. This attack was followed at 1700hrs by a second attack, led by 3/5th Mahrattas, which captured the Pinnacle feature by 1800hrs, paving the way for 3rd Royal Frontier Force to capture the nearby Pimple shortly after midnight. This practically broke through the Italian defences blocking the Dongolas Gorge, repeated Italian counter-attacks failing to dislodge the Indian units from the positions they had conquered. On 16 March, 11th Brigade renewed its attacks against Sanchil and Brig's Peak, only to face a series of determined Italian counter-attacks that were repulsed with bayonets and the heavy use of grenades. Eventually, in the early hours of the 16th, the Italians managed to dislodge part of 2/5th Mahrattas from its position on the south-west corner of Sanchil, provoking an immediate counter-attack that succeeded in regaining the lost positions. By dawn, 1st Royal Fusiliers' attack against the top of Mount Sanchil was successfully repelled, like that of 4/6th Rajputanas' against Brig's Peak. Subsequent attacks also failed due to the complete lack of any kind of support, threatening to repeat the failure of the February battle.

The decisive success came in the 5th Division's sector, where at 0615hrs on 16 March, 2nd West Yorkshires succeeded in seizing Fort Dologorodoc, in spite of stern Italian resistance. The Italians counter-attacked at 1005hrs with extreme violence, the first of a series of assaults lasting until 1330hrs, all repelled with the help of artillery fire. Now able to observe the Keren plain from the captured fort, the Indians started planning the next stage of the operation. On the 17th, 10th Infantry Brigade was brought forward to break through the Italian defences at Mount Sanchil and Brig's Peak, while 5th Division was to use its 9th Brigade to consolidate the positions in the Fort Dologorodoc area and use 29th Brigade to attack to the east and seize Mount Falestoh and Mount Zeban, opening the way to Keren. The attack required the units to be concentrated in the fort area, which was made difficult by the terrain and the heat. The delayed attack started at 0230hrs on the 17th and was marked by progress in the Falestoh area, even though the peak was not actually seized. The attack against Mount Zeban saw 3/2nd Punjabs seize the Zeban Minor feature just to the south of the main peak. To deal with the enemy movements, the Italians launched a series of counter-attacks against Fort Dologorodoc between 18 and 22 March, which were defended strenuously by 2nd West Yorkshires. To make the situation worse for the defenders, continued supply issues prevented the forward troops from receiving food, and some units had to last for 36 hours relying exclusively on field rations. Thanks to air superiority, Platt was kept fully aware of the situation and was eventually able to exploit the weaknesses of the Italian defence. The Italians were determined to hold every position and launched a fanatical series of counter-attacks, but these served only to exhaust their own troops. By 20 March, the Italian forces were down to one-third of their initial strength, General Lorenzini being one of the casualties. Meanwhile, 7th Brigade's action in the north distracted the Italians, further weakening their defences. British and Indian forces regrouped on 19 and 20 March, preparing for the next phase of the battle. The aim now was to break through the Italian positions along the road to Keren in order to make use of the Matilda tanks, which required a push forward from the fort position.

On the night of 16/17 March, Platt threw the last available reserves into the battle for Mount Sanchil and Brig's Peak, 4/10th Baluchs and 3/18th Garhwals attacking without success. On the same night, 29th Brigade attacked Mount Falestoh and Mount Zeban, also to no effect due to tough Italian resistance. Eventually, troops had to be withdrawn. The only achievement came from a close examination of the roadblock, which it was estimated could be overcome within 48 hours. The decisive attack came on 25 March, when 9th and 10th Infantry Brigades attacked up the Dongolas Gorge, both brigades reaching their objectives north

A view of the road leading to Keren and the heights around it. To the left are Cameron Ridge, Mount Samanna, Brig's Peak and Mount Sanchil. To the right are the Pinnacle and Fort Dologorodoc. (From *The Abyssinian Campaigns*, public domain)

of the roadblock in spite of heavy fire while also taking some 500 prisoners. By the afternoon of the 26th, a passage through the roadblock was made, which enabled a composite force of Matilda tanks and Bren carriers – Fletcher Force – to make its way to Keren. Facing this development, General Frusci ordered a withdrawal. On the morning of 27 March, the battle for Keren came to its conclusion, the Italian screening force left behind surrendering and Keren being reported clear of enemy troops by RAF reconnaissance at 0700hrs. One hour later, Fletcher Force entered Keren. The battle had cost the lives of 536 killed and 3,229 wounded amongst Platt's forces, with the Italians losing some 3,000 killed, along with 9,000 of their colonial troops killed, plus 4,500 Italian troops wounded.

THE ATTACK FROM KENYA

If terrain and climatic conditions had proved to be difficult in the north, they were even worse in the south. Most of the terrain dividing Kenya from southern Ethiopia and Italian Somaliland was desert, with high temperatures during the day that dropped to freezing cold during the night. Communications were almost non-existent, all that was available being tracks, which sometimes could not be improved at all and that turned into quagmires after any rain. Considering the lack of oases and the natural barriers provided by rivers, the Italians clearly relied on such obstacles to provide some sort of defence and reckoned that no mechanized or motorized force could attack them. The rainy seasons here added further difficulties, since they extended with various degrees from March to May and October to December, providing very narrow windows of opportunity for an offensive. General Cunningham's situation was made worse by the lack of adequate manpower and resources, due to the needs on other fronts. The offensive from Kenya was made possible thanks to the work of South African engineers, who improved communications and allowed the provision of supplies, water in particular, while accurate maps of the terrain were also provided. Communications, mainly by wireless, were essential to coordinate actions and movements of the various units involved in the operations.

The Italian fort at Mega, where the South African feint took place. (Public domain via Wikimedia Commons)

Advance from Kenya, 15 December 1940–3 March 1941

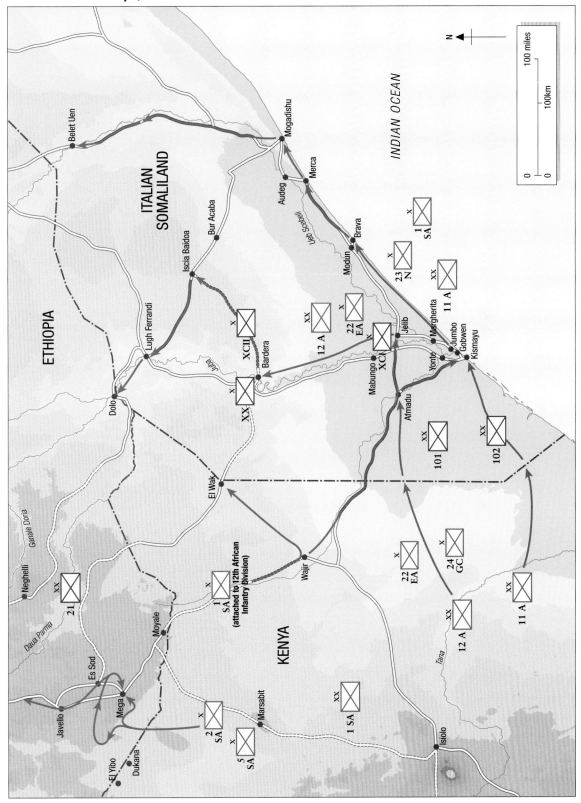

South African troops at Hobok. In the foreground is a Marmon-Herrington armoured car. (Government photographer, public domain, via Wikimedia Commons)

Immediately after relieving General Dickinson early in November 1940, Cunningham examined a plan to seize Kismayu, which led him to suggest a postponement of the start of the offensive until after the spring rains. Wavell agreed, and subsequently South African and African troops started moving towards the frontier in January 1941. During this period, Cunningham decided to impress on the Italian defenders some sort of operational superiority through a series of raids along the border posts. The first raid, carried out at El Wak by 1st South African Brigade, supported by 24th Gold Coast Brigade and 1st South African Light Tank Company, was a complete success, causing the Italians to remove their local commander. The Italian defences had been carefully prepared with a series of advanced strongholds in the middle and lower Juba River area, supported by independent Dubat groups and local bande formations, including the defences of the fords at Bardera and Duglama to the south. A local mobilization had been carried out during 1940 in order to increase the strength of the available units, even though that led to a decrease in their actual fighting power. This was due to the lack of cadres and to the extreme variety of the new recruits, which included teenagers and men in their 70s. Furthermore, Italian Somaliland lacked Italian troops, most of which were found with specialist units (engineers, communications, artillery), which diminished the fighting capability of the defenders. In January 1941, as Comando Settore was redesignated Comando Scacchiere Giuba, the Italian forces in the area amounted to a total of three colonial brigades (XX, XCI and XCII) for a total of 14 colonial battalions, one colonial Carabinieri company, one Raggruppamento Dubat with five groups, two coastal battalions, four bande units – each one some 300–500 strong – one colonial engineer battalion, one Blackshirts battalion and 27 artillery batteries armed with different-calibre guns from the garrison troops. The area had been divided into middle and lower Juba sectors, which met at Dugluma, with the overall Italian defence conceived to assume mostly a passive attitude, but with the possibility of local counter-attacks, focusing on the fords across the Juba River and on Kismayu.

After El Wak, Cunningham focused on the Galla-Sidamo region of Ethiopia, with the aim of supporting the Arbegnoch's activity and starting

Southern Front, 13–22 February 1941

BRITISH	ITALIAN
East Africa Force – Lieutenant-General Alan Cunningham	**Scacchiere Giuba – Lieutenant-General Gustavo Pesenti**
12th African Division, Major-General Godwin-Austen	101 Divisione Coloniale
1st South African Brigade	XX Brigata Coloniale, XCII Brigata Coloniale, XV Brigata Amhara
(1st Transvaal Scottish, 1st Royal Natal Carabineers, 1st Duke	(motorized)
of Edinburgh's Own Rifles, 3rd Armoured Car Company South	102 Divisione Coloniale
African Tank Corps)	XCI Brigata Coloniale (CXCIII, CXCIV, CXCVI)
22nd East African Brigade	Battaglione Costiero V
(1/1st King's African Rifles, 5th King's African Rifles, 1/6th King's	Battaglione Coloniale LXXV, XCIV, CXCV,
African Rifles)	Gruppo Dubat III, VIII
24th Gold Coast Brigade	XLIX Battaglione Amhara
(1st Gold Coast Regiment, 2nd Gold Coast Regiment, 3rd Gold	I battaglione di formazione della marina
Coast Regiment)	VII Battaglione Genio
	CXXII Gruppo misto artiglieria

a local rebellion. In order to achieve that, the 1st South African Division was given the task of moving to the area with its 2nd and 5th Brigades, plus 25th East African Brigade and six irregular Ethiopian companies, which all moved to the east and the west of Lake Rudolf. The concept was to operate from the oasis of Marsabit, moving into Ethiopia at Moyale, a strong defensive position believed to be heavily garrisoned, and across the Chalbi Desert through Dukana, which was expected to be only lightly defended. This led Cunningham to choose south-west East Africa for the first attack. Consequently, on 6 January 1941, the 1st Natal Mounted Rifles with two irregular companies attacked El Yibo, defeating the local bande garrison in two days, which then withdrew. This was followed by 5th Brigade's advance to Dukana, both the 2nd and 5th Brigades crossing the frontier into Ethiopia on 31 January. 2nd Brigade aimed for Gorai, with the 5th heading for Hobok, fighting more than 600km away from their supply centre and enduring the terrible heat. Having failed in the attempt to produce a patriot rising, the concept of the entire operation switched to a bid to secure a line of communication in order to make possible a penetration in depth. This required Moyale to be seized, but first Mega would have to be taken in order to enable the attack on Moyale from the north. Mega was duly attacked on 16 February by 5th Brigade, 2nd Brigade moving against the place two days later, shortly before the surrender of the Italian garrison and the capture of almost 1,000 prisoners. Moyale was then seized without fighting on 22 February by an irregular company, part of 2nd Brigade. The large quantity of water found at Moyale came as a great relief to troops that had endured the heat and lack of water in spite of more than 300 wells dug in the area.

Alternatives were now limited. An attempt to advance north of Lake Rudolf was hindered by the hostility of local tribesmen, which would have required fighting against them, and in Cunningham's view this was

South African field guns in position are firing at Italian defences in the Juba River area, February 1941. (Ibiblio, public domain, via Wikimedia Commons)

THE CROSSING OF THE JUBA RIVER, 19 FEBRUARY 1941 (PP.66–67)

Moving from Marsabit, the most suitable position closest to Nairobi, South African troops (other than the 1st South African Division, the 11th and 12th African Divisions) manoeuvred at first to the north, to attack the Italian positions on the border between Ethiopia and Nigeria. Crossing the Chalbi Desert, the South Africans attacked El Yibo at the end of January 1941, crossing the frontier and switching to the south-east, before attacking Gorai and Mega. This paved the way for the advance to Moyale, which was seized on 22 February. While the actions in the north were in progress, the 11th and 12th African Divisions crossed the Tana River, advancing towards the border, which was only lightly defended by the Italians. On 11 February, the key position of Afmadu was taken, followed three days later by the seizure of Gobwen and Kismayu. On 16 February, 'Yonte Column'

was formed with the HQ of Brigadier Pienaar's 1st South African Infantry Brigade and built around the 1st Transvaal Scottish, and was ordered to reach the ford at Yonte in order to cross the Juba River. Using what the Italians called the 'Ford of Bulo Merere', the South African 1st Transvaal Scottish and 1st Royal Natal Carabineers managed to cross the river **(1)** and, after repulsing Italian attacks, established two different bridgeheads that were soon supported by Marmon Herrington armoured cars of the 3rd South African Armoured Car Company **(2)**, which enabled a further advance inland. This permitted a move into Italian Somaliland, where, on 25 February, the 11th African Division seized Mogadishu unopposed. On the next day, the capture of Bardera marked the end of the Italian presence in Somaliland and paved the way for a South African advance towards Harar.

Two soldiers from the King's African Rifles in the Kenyan bush in 1941. (Charlesdrakew, public domain, via Wikimedia Commons)

a strategically and politically unsuitable move. Instead, he instructed 2nd Brigade to switch to defence, considering the simultaneous advance towards Mogadishu and Wavell's request for troops.

Faced with the Italian withdrawal to the Juba River and the presence of several bande formations, a colonial battalion and a garrison at Kismayu, Cunningham prepared a plan to cross the river. The Italian defences, which included the 14,000-strong 102 Divisione Coloniale on the lower Juba and 6,000-strong 101 Divisione Coloniale on the upper Juba, were deemed not insurmountable by Cunningham, who therefore decided to take the risk and asked Wavell for permission to attack and seize Kismayu. The relevant orders were issued on 2 February. Cunningham was fully aware of the problems caused by the long distances (all in all some 800km between the railheads and the Juba), the lack of equipment and water, and of the poor communications between Kenya and Ethiopia. However, this problem could be solved by using a smaller force of four brigades instead of the planned six, which Cunningham considered sufficient to defeat the Italians anyway. Cunningham's plan saw 12th African Division (with 1st South African, 22nd East Africa and 24th Gold Coast Brigade) move against Afmadu on 11 February, with 1st South African Brigade then turning south to seize the Gobwen airfield before crossing the Juba River and establishing a bridgehead at Jumbo. At the same time, the 24th Gold Coast Brigade was to advance north of Kismayu to prevent the Italian reinforcements from Gobwen reaching the area from the north. 11th African Division, with 23rd Nigerian Brigade, would move to the south, advancing at a subsequent stage to Kismayu, taking advantage of the Italian defences being distracted by 12th African Division's activity. No written orders were issued to preserve the secrecy of the plan while a deception was staged using wireless activity to persuade the Italians of the presence of an Australian division near the frontier. In the situation that Kismayu resisted and could not be seized within ten days, the troops had to withdraw but, in case of success, Cunningham planned on seizing Mogadishu and advancing north along the Juba River.

Cunningham's offensive started on 2 February with a series of air attacks carried out by the South African Air Force against Italian airfields at Gobwen, Afmadu and Dif. The extent and intensity of the attacks eventually compelled the Afmadu garrison to abandon its position and withdraw, enabling 22nd East African Brigade to seize the place unopposed on 11 February. This made it possible for the 24th Gold Coast Brigade to advance some 100km to reach Bulo Erillo, where they encountered strong Italian resistance, which was eventually overcome and 141 prisoners were taken at the cost of heavy losses amongst officers. In the meantime, 1st South African Brigade under Brigadier Pienaar approached Gobwen, remaining under cover in order to achieve maximum surprise. Overly cautious, Pienaar failed to detect that the Italians were clearly evacuating Kismayu. Moving in the early hours of 14 February, 1st South African Brigade was able to seize Gobwen without a fight but was unable to intercept the withdrawing Italians. A first bridgehead on the Juba was then established. As 23rd Nigerian Brigade was unavailable, Cunningham ordered 22nd East African Brigade to move from Afmadu to Kismayu, which it entered on the 14th, just after the Italian escape, six days before the date set to complete the first part of the offensive.

With the Italian defences now in a clear state of disarray, Cunningham decided to dash forward and cross the Juba. The first bridgehead at Gobwen soon became untenable, as the pontoon bridge established there was destroyed and the units drew considerable fire from the Italian defenders, who relied on the 200m-wide river. Pienaar soon found another suitable crossing place some 16km to the north, at Yonte, where a company of 1st Royal Natal Carabineers crossed the river on 17 February, establishing a bridgehead that was expanded the next day by 1st Transvaal Scottish, who repulsed an Italian counter-attack. A pontoon bridge was laid on the 19th, enabling the 1st South African Brigade to race to Jumbo, on the coast, which was seized, with the capture of the entire garrison. On the same day, the 24th

South African troops from the King's African Rifles entering Kismayu on 14 February 1941. (From *The Abyssinian Campaigns*, public domain)

Gold Coast Brigade crossed the Juba at Mabungo, north of Jelib, which was the last important objective left to be seized in the area. Jelib was attacked by the 24th Gold Coast Brigade from the north and 1st South African Brigade from the south, with 22nd East African Brigade being sent to the south-east along the coast to cut off the Mogadishu road. As Jelib fell on 22 February, the disintegration of the Italian forces in the Juba area was completed, with minimal losses due to the lack of any coherent Italian opposition. The swift success enabled Cunningham to start the advance towards Mogadishu, which he now reckoned would not be heavily defended, and start considering the removal of troops from Kenya for other purposes. Also on 22 February, Cunningham suggested to Wavell that Berbera be seized in order to shorten the line of supply, to which Wavell replied that this would be done by a force from Aden. On 19 February, the first sea convoy from Mombasa arrived at Kismayu, which, in spite of the difficulties in using the harbour, enabled the advance to continue. 23rd Nigerian Brigade reached the Mabungo bridgehead, only to be repulsed on 22 February by an Italian counter-attack. At the same time, 22nd East African Brigade advanced from Jelib to Modun, which was bombarded by sea. Then the 23rd Nigerian Brigade took the lead, reaching Mogadishu on 25 February without encountering opposition, while 1st South African Brigade went into reserve. The swift advance, which covered some 380km in just three days, enabled a major reorganization which saw the 12th African Division taking command of the 21st East African Brigade and 24th Gold Coast Brigade, both of which had been advancing to the north since the end of the month because of the difficulties encountered with the harbour at Kismayu. Having reached Mogadishu – where a large amount of fuel and lubricants was captured – the advance halted, the harbour being closed due to the lack of the necessary equipment to sweep it for sea mines.

THE DRIVE TO AMBA ALAGI

By 22 February, the Italian 102 Divisione Coloniale had practically ceased to exist and the Italian front had crumbled. To deal with this, Comando Scacchiere Giuba ordered 101 Divisione Coloniale to withdraw into Ethiopia to the line of the Webi Scebeli River, forming a defensive line with other withdrawing Italian units against the enemy forces advancing from the west and the south. As the withdrawal started, Comando Superiore Africa Orientale ordered 101 Divisione Coloniale to withdraw to Neghelli in the Galla-Sidamo region, leaving the task to form the defence line in the Harar region to the other retreating troops. The redeployment was complete by early March, with the Italians suffering the loss of most of their colonial troops, many of whom deserted, along with

British victory parade after the capture of Asmara. The Indian troops pictured here paraded through the town to mark the advance into Eritrea and its actual seizure. (Photo by Bettmann/Getty Images)

Mounted on a charger and surrounded by the loyal warriors of his bodyguard, Emperor Halle Selassie nears the end of his 200-mile trek through mountain and jungle to the headquarters camp he set up in the kingdom retaken by British and Ethiopian forces from the shattered Italian armies. (Photo by Bettmann/Getty Images)

the loss of vehicles and equipment due to the poor roads. Vast distances and the almost complete lack of communications now proved to be the best ally for the Italians because, despite the issues these caused to themselves, they also hindered the advance of Cunningham's forces. The Italian redeployment was actually Cunningham's best achievement, as he ordered his commanders to make the Italians believe that the main advance would aim for Neghelli and not, as it did, for the Harar region in order to link up with the forces landing in British Somaliland from Aden. This was a remarkable accomplishment, even with the scant opposition encountered, considering the supply issues and the distances that were covered in a relatively small amount of time, the distance between Mogadishu and Jijiga being more than 1,000km covered by a single road, of which only one-third was usable for motorized vehicles.

On 11 March, 1st South African Brigade and 22nd East African Brigade came under the command of 11th African Division, along with 23rd Nigerian Brigade, which started its advance supported by RAF offensive reconnaissance, with reports indicating that the Italians were withdrawing to Jijiga. On 16 March, as two battalions from the Aden garrison landed at Berbera, the LXX Brigata Coloniale melted away, enabling the re-conquest of British Somaliland and access to supplies from Berbera harbour, reducing the distance to supply bases by roughly 800km. On 23 March, the 2nd South

British infantry, in high spirits after entering the Ethiopian capital of Addis Ababa, celebrate the final victory over the Italians. (Photo by Haynes Archive/Popperfoto via Getty Images)

African Brigade arrived from Mombasa and Brigadier Chater was appointed Governor of Somaliland. Jijiga was seized on 17 March by the 23rd Nigerian Brigade without opposition, the Italians holding the pass leading to the Ethiopian highlands. The Italian positions and lack of troops required that the brigade wait for reinforcements from 1st South African Brigade, which only reached Jijiga on 23 March, before attempting to attack. However, as the Italians had started to withdraw, the attack was started two days before the arrival of 1st South African

Emperor Haile Selassie rides in the back of an open-topped, captured Italian car into Addis Ababa as he returns to Ethiopia from exile. (Photo by Keystone/Hulton Archive/Getty Images)

Brigade, and the pass was successfully seized. The Italians then took up the defence of another pass, though they were quickly overcome there too. At this point, the Italians attempted to declare Harar an open city, hoping to be allowed to withdraw, but 11th Division commander General Wetherall disabused them of this notion and sent his armoured cars forward. They entered Harar on 26 March, taking 572 prisoners and ending the first part of 23rd Nigerian Brigade's advance, totalling some 1,600km in just 32 days.

Engaged in pursuing the withdrawing Italians, Cunningham had the option to advance to Diredawa and, from there, to Addis Ababa by either the direct or indirect route. The latter was chosen in order to avoid obstructions on the direct path. On 29 March, the Transvaal Scottish entered Diredawa at the request of the Italians, as their colonial troops were being attacked by native deserters and they wanted British troops to deal with the unrest. Having cleared the road obstructions, the advance was only temporarily halted by a lack of fuel and was resumed by 22nd East African Brigade, which took the lead and reached the Awash River. In spite of the barrier presented by the river and the Italian defence, the brigade managed to cross it and establish a bridgehead, cutting off the defenders and enabling the further advance on Addis Ababa. As early as 30 March, Cunningham believed they could seize Addis Ababa without much difficulty, so he turned his concern towards the possible problems that the large number of colonial deserters could create. This prompted General Wavell to contact Amedeo d'Aosta to try to deal with the situation. The message sent by the Italians on 3 April, detailing the necessary arrangement in order to avoid disorder, basically guaranteed that no real opposition would be encountered with the seizure of Addis Ababa. On 5 April, the pontoon bridge across the Awash was completed and the advance was resumed, the Italians once again asking that the British promptly seize the city to deal with the local unrest caused by looting. While the rest of Italian Somaliland was occupied, mainly to restore order and prevent unrest, the seizure of Addis Ababa put an end to the first part of Cunningham's campaign in Ethiopia, which had been characterized by the extreme mobility and speed of the British troops in taking advantage of the collapse of Italian units.

Closing the pincer, Addis Ababa and Amba Alagi, 23 March–21 June 1941

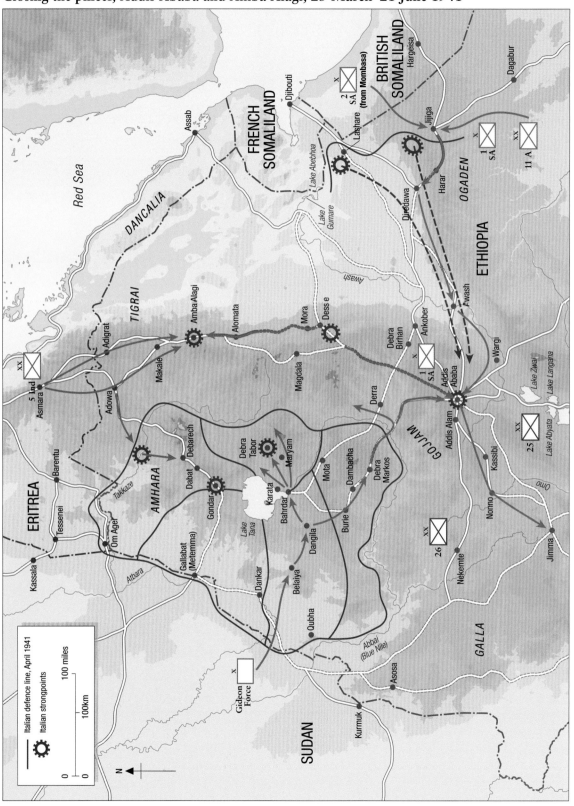

Red Sea

DANCALIA

FRENCH SOMALILAND

BRITISH SOMALILAND

Djibouti

Assab

Hargeisa

Dagabur

Djibouti

2 SA (from Mombasa)

Lashare

Jijiga

1 SA

11 A

Lake Abebhoa

OGADEN

Lake Gumare

Harar

ETHIOPIA

Diredawa

TIGRAI

Adigrat

Amba Alagi

Alomata

Mora

Dess e

Ewash

Awash

Ankober

Wargi

Makale

Magdala

Debra Birhan

Adowa

1 SA

Addis Ababa

ERITREA

5 Ind

Asmara

Derra

Addis Alam

Lake Zwai

Lake Langana

GOJJAM

Debarech

Debra Tabor

Maryam

25

Lake Abyata

Barentu

Debra Markos

Kassibi

AMHARA

Dabat

Mota

Dambacha

Om Ager

Gondar

Karata

Burie

Nonno

Jimma

Tessenei

Lake Tana

Bahrdar

Dangila

Omo

Kassala

Gallabat (Metemma)

Nekemte

Dankar

26

Belaiya

Takkaze

Atbara

Qubha

Abbai (Blue Nile)

Asosa

GALLA

Gideon Force

SUDAN

Kurmuk

Legend

Italian defence line, April 1941

Italian strongpoints

100 miles

100km

0

0

N

74

Italian forces, May 1941

COMANDO FORZE ARMATE AFRICA ORIENTALE ITALIANA
Commander-in-Chief: Lieutenant-General Pietro Gazzera
Scacchiere Sud – Lieutenant-General Pietro Gazzera
Zona Sinistra – Omo, Lieutenant-General Antonio Tissi
21 Divisione Coloniale, Brigadier-General Ettore Caffaratti
24 Divisione Coloniale, Brigadier-General Emanuele Beraudo
di Pralomo
25 Divisione Coloniale, Brigadier-General Amedeo Liberati
101 Divisione Coloniale (rebuilt), Brigadier-General
Alfredo Baccari

Zona Centro, Lieutenant-General Ettore Scala
22 Divisione Coloniale, Brigadier-General Guido Pialorsi

Zona Dabus – Dimessa, Lieutenant-General Carlo De Simone

Scacchiere Ovest – Lieutenant-General Guglielmo Nasi
Piazzaforte Gondar, Lieutenant-General Guglielmo Nasi
Piazzaforte Uolchefit, Lieutenant-Colonel Mario Gonella
Piazzaforte Debra Tabor, Colonel Ignazio Angelici
Settore Danaclia, Brigadier-General Pietro Piacentini
Guarnigione Tio-Assab-Rahesta, Commander Guglielmo Bolla
(Royal Italian Navy)
Presidio Sardo-Dobi, Colonel Umberto Raugei
Settore Elidar-Manda, Brigadier-General Luigi Frusci

The seizure of Addis Ababa coincided with Emperor Haile Selassie's return to the throne and the peak of rebel activity in Ethiopia and of Wingate's campaign. In 1939, Wavell had created the premise for an organized insurrection in Italian-occupied Ethiopia, giving the task to Lieutenant-Colonel Daniel Sandford, who, assisted by the Sudan Defence Force, formed a military mission to Ethiopia named 'Fuse 101' for the purpose of organizing and spreading the already existing Ethiopian revolt. After the creation of a Sudan Defence Force battalion, Platt ordered Sandford on 21 June 1940 to enter Ethiopia to coordinate the insurgents' activity. On 12 August that year, Haile Selassie arrived at Khartoum with the now re-designated Mission 101, and Sandford created an insurgent base in the Gojjam region. Wingate's task, as he arrived at Khartoum on 6 November, was to liaise between Wavell, Selassie and Sandford, but he soon turned his task and his staff into a full command and flew to Gojjam on 20 November to meet Sandford. This led to the creation of a proper military force, known as Gideon Force, comprising 2,000 Sudanese troops from the Sudanese Frontier Battalion and the restored 2nd Ethiopian Battalion with personnel formerly part of the Ethiopian army, all led by 70 British officers and NCOs. They would be joined by about 1,000 guerrillas and be supported by Lieutenant Anthony Simond's Beghemder Force (named after the region south of Lake Tana), which acted independently. The first step was to establish Selassie's headquarters at Belaiya, south-west of Lake Tana, where he arrived on 6 February 1941 after returning to his country. Two days later, Wingate was made commander of the British and Ethiopian forces, Sandford being relegated to the role of liaison officer. At the end of the month, Wingate's 1,500 men moved from Gallabat into Ethiopia to the south of Lake Tana, while Beghemder Force advanced to the north. They both faced Brigata Coloniale, which attempted to set up defences at Burie and Mankusa before withdrawing. The advance of Gideon Force was slowed by the defeat of the 2nd Ethiopian Battalion during an encounter with withdrawing Italian forces. Wingate forced the Italians to continue their retreat before occupying Dambacha (south of Tana) on 6 March. At this point, the Italians, realizing they had underestimated Wingate's strength, put up a stiff resistance, which brought Platt's and Cunningham's victorious advance to an end. This enabled Wingate to resume his offensive, followed by Haile Selassie, and seize Debra Markos on 3 April, the first step to the restoration of the Ethiopian government. While Wingate carried

Indian troops advancing towards the Amba Alagi mountain to defeat the last Italian resistance in the area. (Ibiblio, public domain, via Wikimedia Commons)

on with his irregular warfare, both the British government and General Platt got cold feet about guerrilla warfare and the role of the emperor, wanting it made clear that it was the British who had returned him to Addis Ababa. Even though Addis Ababa was actually seized on 6 April, Haile Selassie did not enter the city until 5 May, sending a clear signal that his rule was restored and that the Ethiopians were able to fight the Italians. While Gideon Force continued to harass the withdrawing Italian troops, the Ethiopians created formations that contributed to the ultimate defeat of Italian forces in East Africa.

As the situation progressed in southern and western Ethiopia, Italian forces attempted a last coordinated resistance in Eritrea against the British following the withdrawal from Keren. Between the end of March and early April, the Italians withdrew from Keren towards Asmara, where the last available reserves, mostly elements from the 10 Reggimento Granatieri, were brought in from Addis Ababa to form a line of defence at Ad Teclesan. By 28 March, the advancing British troops seized one of the peaks forming the defensive position at Ad Teclesan, thus endangering the Italian forces, which comprised three colonial battalions and three Blackshirts companies. While the battle for the approach to Asmara raged, the Comando Superiore Africa Orientale gave the order to surrender Asmara to spare civilian lives, to defend Massawa as a redoubt, to focus on Amba Alagi, where Amedeo d'Aosta had escaped from Addis Ababa, and for the blocking of every access to the last redoubts at Gondar and in the areas of Galla-Sidamo, where the final available forces were to resist as long as possible. On 31 March, Ad Teclesan was seized by 9th Indian Infantry Brigade, which took 460 prisoners. The next day, Asmara surrendered without a fight, paving the way for the advance inland. On that same day, three of the six Italian destroyers at Massawa put to sea, one of them sinking at once and the remaining two returning to base. Eventually, the remaining five destroyers set out to raid Port Sudan. Before reaching their objective, they were attacked by Swordfish from the Royal Navy aircraft carrier *Eagle*, which sank two of them and forced two others to be abandoned, while the fifth one was later scuttled. With Massawa no longer posing a threat to the Red Sea route, and considering the success achieved on the battlefield, Wavell decided to move 4th Indian Division back to Egypt, leaving in Eritrea the 7th Brigade Group under the command of General Heath, which reconnoitred the roads leading to Adowa and Adigrat while preparing to attack Massawa. By 8 April, 10th Indian Brigade and the French 'Brigade d'Orient' had closed the ring around Massawa and, after offering surrender which was refused, 7th Brigade attacked against resolute Italian opposition. Meanwhile, 10th Brigade, supported

A group of Ethiopian soldiers. Following the victory at Amba Alagi, their forces provided great support to the British and South African troops mopping up the remaining Italian resistance in East Africa. (Imperial War Museum, K 325)

by B Squadron of 4th Royal Tank Regiment, broke through the western defences and the Free France troops broke through in the south-west. Massawa surrendered early in the afternoon, with 9,590 Italians being taken prisoner. The harbour was soon available for bringing in supplies by sea, while the Massawa–Asmara railway line was operational from 27 April. By early May, both Platt's and Cunningham's troops could rely on relatively short supply lines linked to the harbours at Massawa and Berbera.

Amedeo d'Aosta, facing defeat, had the remaining Italian forces withdraw to the redoubts and positioned himself in the Amba Alagi redoubt, hoping for a protracted resistance, a questionable choice because the Gondar area

A column of Italian vehicles abandoned along a road leading to Amba Alagi. This was the last important redoubt in the area, which the Italian commander, Amedeo d'Aosta, chose to be his final defence. (Ibiblio, public domain, via Wikimedia Commons)

Italian forces at Amba Alagi, 1–17 May 1941

Settore Falagà, Lieutenant-Colonel Postiglione
XLIII Brigata Coloniale (XLI, LIII)

Settore Toselli
XXVI Battaglione Coloniale
Battaglione Carabinieri Reali

Battaglione Azzurro (air force personnel)
II, III/60 Reggimento Artiglieria
Battaglione Mitraglieri 'Granatieri di Savoia'

Settore Togorà, Colonel Largajolli
Gruppo Bande Polizia Africa Italiana

offered better possibilities for a lengthy defence. On 7 April, Comando Scacchiere Amba Alagi was formed under General Frusci at Dessie and General Valletti-Borgnini at Amba Alagi. The Dessie redoubt had three Blackshirts battalions (III, XI and XII), the 'Assab' garrison battalion, a naval personnel battalion, the XVIII Battaglione Genio (engineers), three colonial battalions (XXXII, XLVI and LXX), the XI Gruppo Squadroni Cavalleria and one colonial Banda. This represented the bulk of the Italian forces available, with Amba Alagi itself being lightly defended by the XLIII Brigata Coloniale, four colonial battalions and the 211 Reggimento Fanteria d'Africa, along with elements from the Polizia Africa Italiana and remnants of the Divisione 'Granatieri di Savoia'. Following the seizure of Massawa, a pincer movement was organized against Amba Alagi, with 5th Indian Division (now led by General Mayne) attacking from the north with Fletcher Force, 29th Indian Brigade plus two battalions from the 9th and 10th Brigades, and one Commando unit. From the south, the attack was led by the 1st South African Brigade Group, the entire operation being actively supported by Arbegnoch forces. A swift advance from the south enabled the prompt seizure of a dominating feature on 19 April, which the Italians unsuccessfully attempted to retake. On 22 April, Pienaar attacked the main Italian positions, supported by a large band of patriots, the flank of the Italian defences being stormed by the 1st Royal Natal Carabineers. Dessie fell on 26 April, yielding some 8,000 prisoners at the cost of nine killed and 30 wounded. Italian losses also included large numbers of deserters.

General Mayne made a feint attack against the central and eastern Italian defences at Amba Alagi, actually assaulting the less approachable western defences. On 2 May, Fletcher Force attacked the Falaga Pass in the east without success, while in the centre, 3/18th Garhwal made a demonstration. At the same time, 6/13th Frontier Force and 3/2nd Punjabs attacked the Italian positions to the west, soon seizing three dominating features and approaching Amba Alagi. Any further advance from that area was soon halted by stern Italian defence, and Mayne, having been informed by Fletcher Force of the weakness of the Italian forces in the eastern sector, decided to switch his main advance there, providing Colonel Fletcher with the HQ of 9th Indian Brigade. On 8 May, Cunningham put his 1st South African Brigade at Mayne's disposal, enabling an attack on the positions to the west of the Falaga Pass, which were also attacked by a large, organized group of patriots on 13 May. By the 15th, the remnants of the Italian troops had been pushed back into Amba Alagi, Forte Toselli protecting its eastern approaches being no longer a suitable target and therefore not being attacked. On 16 May, negotiations were opened for an armistice, the Italian requesting that Amedeo d'Aosta remain at

Amba Alagi as a non-belligerent governor to ensure the protection of the Italian nationals. However, this would not be conceded by the British, and the Italians eventually agreed to a full surrender 'with the honours of war', which would become a recurring theme in Italian attitudes in the region. The British agreed to this pageantry in order not to delay the surrender. On 19 May, the 5,000-strong Italian garrison duly marched past a guard of honour before being disarmed, with Amedeo d'Aosta surrendering himself and his personal staff to General Mayne the next day. He was then taken to meet General Platt, and with that, the surrender of Amba Alagi practically put an end to the East African campaign. All that was left was to surround and eliminate the remaining Italian strongholds, which were mostly concentrated in the area of the lakes and around Gondar. The campaign was practically won inside two months thanks to the organization, determination, accurate preparation and training of troops who endured the most difficult conditions and performed exceptionally under stress. The British losses suffered were minimal, especially in comparison with the casualties of the Italians, whose numerical superiority counted for nothing.

MOPPING UP

Amedeo d'Aosta's surrender at Amba Alagi was merely a symbolic act, summarizing the Italian defeat. The threat of an Italian combined offensive against Egypt had long gone, and with the victories achieved by Platt and Cunningham, there was no longer a threat against the Red Sea or the British colonies in the region. This, coupled with Selassie's increased numbers which helped in the mopping-up operations, enabled Wavell to transfer troops from East Africa to deal with the worrying situation in North Africa and Greece. The remnants of the Italian forces were now scattered and, even though General Gazzera had been appointed by Mussolini on 19 May as superior commander in East Africa (Comandante Superiore Forze Armate

A South African 25-pdr gun position in the Amba Alagi area, May 1941. (Ibiblio, public domain, via Wikimedia Commons)

The battle of the Lakes, Addis Ababa and Amba Alagi, 9 April–5 June 1941

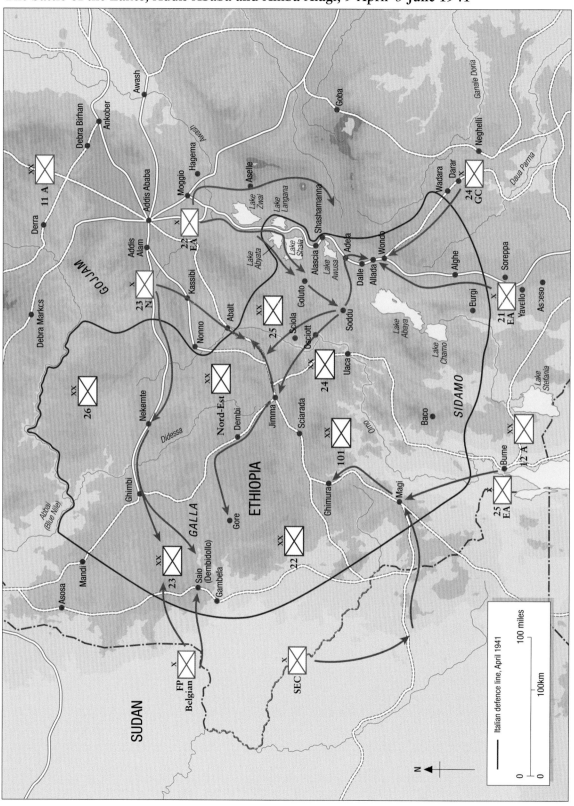

Amedeo d'Aosta, second from the left, after his surrender on 19 May 1941 to General Mayne (left), moments before being conceded the honours of war. (Australian War Memorial, 007946)

Africa Orientale Italiana) and regent of the Italian government in East Africa, there was no longer a proper unified command. Each stronghold simply resisted, with the aim of lasting as long as possible before the unavoidable surrender. Scattered pockets of Italian troops to the west of French Somaliland and in northern Italian Somaliland had surrendered one-by-one since the end of April. Assab, on the Red Sea, surrendered with the remnants of the garrisons in the nearby area on 11 June, along with the last Italian troops in northern Somaliland.

The most defendable strongholds were found to the north and south of Lake Tana, a mountainous area that was hard to access but easy to defend. The Italian idleness and their withdrawal into the strongholds granted the British commanders time to prepare their operations and plan a series of coordinated attacks that could be carried out with the minimum of forces. In the area south and west of Addis Ababa, the Galla-Sidamo region, General Gazzera had at his disposal the headquarters of four colonial divisions and two colonial brigades, five Blackshirts and 25 colonial battalions, four Gruppo Banda and one Gruppo Squadroni Cavalleria Coloniale, along with other troops. Since early April, General Cunningham had prepared a plan to advance towards Jimma, to the south-west of Addis Ababa, and to the lakes area from the east, foreseeing a subsequent advance from the north towards the Yavello–Neghelli area in order to clear the last corner of the crumbling Italian empire. The plan was temporarily set aside as, following Wavell's request to clear the Addis Ababa–Asmara road, priority was given to the seizure of Amba Alagi. At the conclusion of this operation, Cunningham had to face the fact that the forces available were not sufficient for the multiple tasks and that the situation had changed in the meantime, with 22nd African Brigade at Addis Ababa and 21st African Brigade already at Yavello, while 24th Gold Coast Brigade was at Neghelli. This led to a postponement of the advance on Jimma, which had Cunningham developing a double action plan with both the 11th and 12th African Divisions intended to clear the lakes region, moving to the west and south of Addis Ababa. This would secure a direct line of communications between Kenya and Addis Ababa. The 25th East African Brigade, intended to support this move from the Lake Rudolf area, could not move due to difficult terrain and adverse weather conditions. Terrain, weather (the rainy season started here in April) and poor communications apart, Cunningham's main problem was supply, since the troops in the Addis Ababa area were being supplied via Berbera.

Not surprisingly, the first step proved disastrous. On 11 April, 22nd East Africa Brigade moved to Aselle, relying on inaccurate intelligence and Italian maps. It soon found that there were not many Italians in the area and that the roads were in fact impassable tracks, so the brigade started to advance to Lake Zwai, just south of Addis Ababa. After a clash with Italian troops in the northern lakes area, the brigade started to reconnoitre the area in a more accurate way, enabling 11th African Division to join in. On 9 May, the advance started towards Lake Shala, to the north of Shashamanna, facing little Italian opposition and dealing with persistent rains, flooding and all sorts of other obstacles. On 14 May, Shashamanna was reached, the advancing troops moving on to Dalle some 60km to the south, close to the crossroads leading to Yavello and Neghelli. The link-up with 24th Gold Coast Brigade was not an easy matter, however, since the latter had to struggle against the weather and strong Italian defences at Wadara, about halfway between Neghelli and Dalle. These defences were eventually overcome on 10 May, enabling a further advance to Wondo, just to the south of Dalle, which was reached on 25 May. At this point, the Italian opposition was causing far fewer problems than the appalling weather and the terrain. The advance of 21st East African Brigade from Yavello was slowed down by Italian resistance at Alghe, about halfway to Dalle, and by insufficient supplies. In view of the situation, Cunningham ordered the 11th African Division to advance to Soddu (west of Shashamanna, between the two groups of lakes), where it was to link up with 12th African Division advancing from the south. This would free the former and enable it to advance to Jimma. However, this soon turned out to be an illusion as 12th Division's advance from Neghelli was slowed down by the terrain. This compelled Cunningham to order 11th Division to advance towards Soddu and Jimma regardless, while 12th Division was to clear and secure the rear area. Advancing from Shashamanna on 21 May, 22nd East Africa Brigade clashed with a group of Italians supported by tanks, six of which were destroyed by Sergeant N. G. Leakey of 1/6th African Rifles, who was awarded a posthumous Victoria Cross. Soddu was seized on 23 May, the commanders and staffs of the 25 and 101 Divisione Coloniale being taken prisoner. As a consequence, 21 and 24 Brigata Coloniale were ordered to withdraw south, towards Lake Abaya, to reach the Omo River, taking any Italian nationals with them. Only 24 Brigata Coloniale and the Italian nationals managed to reach the Omo, before surrendering in mid-June as it was unable to get across. By then, the total number of Italian prisoners taken west of the river totalled 18,396.

With the area east of the lakes being now practically cleared, the next step was to advance to Jimma in order to link Sudan with Ethiopia. The 23rd Nigerian Brigade was chosen for the seizure of Jimma, reorganized and reinforced for the purpose. The more than 100m-wide River Omo posed the first obstacle, the Italian defences to the west being the second.

Comando Truppe Amara, 8 September 1941

Ridotto Uolchefit
Caposaldo di Ualag
Caposaldo di Culquaber, with: XXII Brigata Coloniale (LXXVII, LXXXI), I Gruppo Bande di Confine, XIV Gruppo Squadroni

Cavalleria Coloniale
Caposaldo di Celgà
Caposaldo di Tucul Dinghià

The plan was to have 22nd East African Brigade cross the river at Sciola, east of Jimma, while 23rd Nigerian Brigade crossed to the north at Abalti. Whichever of the two managed to establish a firm bridgehead would be helped and assisted by the other. A first, rushed attempt to attack Sciola was made on 31 May, without results. On 1 June, all attempts to cross the Omo failed because of a strong current, but on the next day a suitable place was found and a first bridgehead was built by 4 June, enabling the Italian positions to be attacked, which surrendered on the 5th, with 1,100 prisoners being taken. The crossing at Abalti followed a similar pattern. After a first attempt on 31 May, a second attempt succeeded on 4 and 5 June, leading to an assault on the Italian defences, which did not put up much resistance. By 6 June, the Italian units withdrew towards Jimma, leaving behind 2,850 prisoners. Cunningham was in no rush to seize Jimma, but the Italians preceded him. Shortly after the Omo crossing, General Gazzera declared Jimma an open city and tried to hand it over to Cunningham, who declined any responsibility for the Italian civilians in spite of the fact that preparations for a swift takeover had been made. On 20 June, Cunningham ordered 22nd East African Brigade to advance west of Jimma, which was seized on the next day without a fight, a grand total of 15,000 prisoners being taken. During this time, the 23rd Nigerian Brigade had been advancing to the west of Addis Ababa and reached Ghimbi by the end of June, capturing the last Italian forces east of the Didessa River and practically cleaning up the entire area, which was now being swarmed by Arbegnoch fighters. After the seizure of Dembi on 27 June, the last Italian units in the area – 23 and 26 Divisione Coloniale – kept withdrawing westwards, evading the British forces, which were slowed down by the terrain. To prevent their prolonged resistance, General Platt used a composite force made up of 2/6th King's African Rifles and a Belgian contingent from the Congo, which had been advancing into Ethiopia since the end of March and deployed at the Sudan border to prevent the Italians from escaping. Eventually, on 27 June, General Platt asked the Belgian contingent to attack the Italian forces whenever possible; their commander, General Gilliaert, moved at once, attacking on 3 July. General Gazzera's response was to negotiate a surrender, which was to include the customary request of the honours of war. Gilliaert agreed, Gazzera surrendering on 6 July with the remnants of his troops, a total of 2,944 Italians, 1,535 colonial troops and some 2,000 troops with the Bande, thus ending the battle of the Lakes and the last operations in the Galla-Sidamo area.

What remained was the last, best-organized and strongest Italian redoubt to the north of Addis Ababa and Lake Tana, that at Gondar. Since the outbreak of the war, the main concern of the Italian forces in the area had been to prevent a large-scale patriotic insurgency, a situation made worse following the British offensive and the penetration into the area of

The end at Gondar, 27 September–27 November 1941

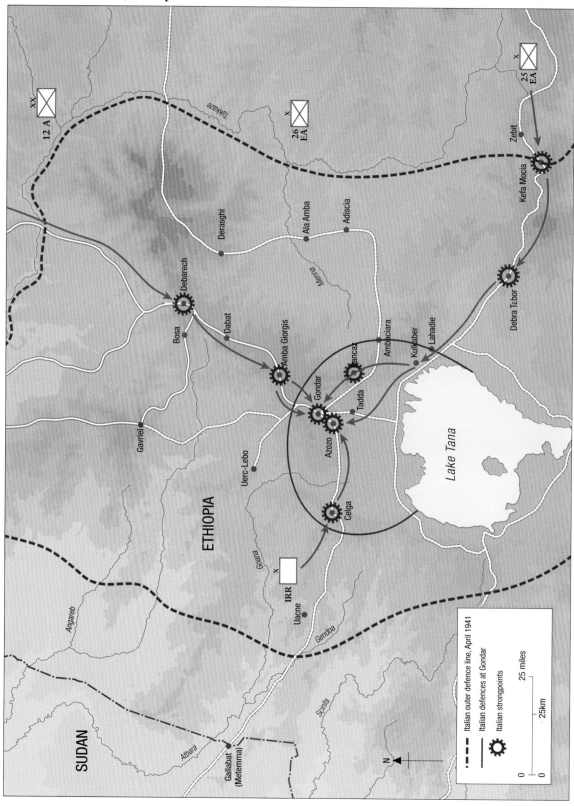

Colonel Gonella talking with the British brigadier who accepted the surrender of his forces at the Wolchefit Pass on 27 September 1941. (Photo by Mirrorpix/Mirrorpix via Getty Images)

Colonel Sandford's mission. With many supply columns being attacked, the scattered Italian garrisons were practically isolated, which prompted the Italians to start a series of operations against the Arbegnoch. Early in February 1941, the commander of Scacchiere Ovest, General Nasi, instructed the garrison to withdraw to the area around Gondar in order to ensure a better defence. This movement was completed in early March, when Nasi realized that the Italian position in East Africa was already doomed and opted for a prolonged resistance in the area around Gondar. This was proved right on 30 March, when Amedeo d'Aosta instructed Nasi to form strong defensive positions in the Gondar area, which was

Italian troops at the Wolchefit Pass near Gondar surrender, marching past a guard of honour from the King's African Rifles. (Photo by Mirrorpix/Mirrorpix via Getty Images)

85

East Africa Command, 15 September 1941

East Africa Force was disbanded on 15 September 1941 and replaced by East Africa Command under direct command of the War Office
East Africa Command – Lieutenant General Sir William Platt
Eritrea Area (administrative)
Northern Area: 12th (African) Division, Major-General C. C.

Fowkes (Ethiopia, British Somaliland)
Central Area: 11th (African) Division, Major-General Harry Wetherall (Italian Somaliland, Uganda, Kenya)
Southern Area: Major-General G. R. Smallwood (Nyasaland, Northern Rhodesia)

intended to support the Amba Alagi position. Between March and May 1941, groups of isolated Italian units along with stragglers made their way to the Gondar area, thereby strengthening the defences. By then, Nasi could rely on some 17,000 Italian and 23,000 colonial troops, which formed two redoubts to the north and south of Gondar, as well as the local defences. The northern redoubt, at the Wolchefit Pass and Debarech, with about 5,000 troops under the orders of Lieutenant-Colonel Mario Gonnella, defended the northern approaches. It relied mostly on the natural position of the Wolchefit Pass, which posed a serious obstacle to any enemy force approaching from the north. The southern stronghold (led by Colonel Ignazio Angelini) at Debra Tabor blocked the road from Dessie and was defended by some 6,000 men protected by a barbed wire belt 7km wide. The position had no natural defences and was chosen initially for purely political reasons, the defenders eventually relying on the natural obstacles to the north of Debra Tabor, near Lake Tana, mainly at Kulkaber. Gondar itself had two separate strongholds and four external ones. The force holding the Gondar stronghold complex, commanded by Colonel Fortunato Marinelli, was 30,000-strong, with seven Italian and six colonial battalions, 13 field gun batteries and a reserve of five colonial battalions and a series of Gruppo Banda.

The approach to Gondar dictated the outline of the plan of attack. From February 1941, Wingate's forces had penetrated the area, moving from Gallabat to Chilga, some 50km west of Gondar, where a garrison controlled the area. Road conditions ruled the approaches. Re-deploying large numbers of troops to Chilga would have taken too long and, for this reason, the approach from the west was excluded. There was only a poor road to the south of Gondar, which, to the south-east of Lake Tana, turned into a mountain

An Ethiopian repatriation convoy. Ethiopian prisoners of war who were being released by the British are pushing one of the more than 120 trucks which transported them from a British internment camp in Sudan to Dessie. (Photo by Universal History Archive/UIG via Getty images)

A group of Ethiopian soldiers crossing the Omo River in May 1941, before the last Italian resistance west of Amba Alagi surrendered. (British Army, public domain, via Wikimedia Commons)

track leading to Dessie, some 180km away. This was considered unsuitable and unable to support any large-scale operation. This left the approach from the north, where the British forces could rely on the relatively good road leading from Asmara to Gondar (which secured the flow of supplies from the sea). The north was thus not just the most favourable approach, but also the only possible one even taking into account the natural defence area of the Wolchefit Pass and the mountains rising to Amba Giorgis. Taking the Italian defences into account, General Platt decided not to rush things and dealt first with the necessary reorganization of the forces in the area. From April, the task of fighting the Italians in the Gondar region was left to the patriots, while the areas to the south (Galla-Sidamo) and to the north were being cleared in order to make troops available. The rainy weather impeded air activity, which eventually focused on providing support to the early operations, aimed at the Debra Tabor–Gondar road. This was Major A. C. Simonds' task from April, carried out with No. 2 Operational Centre and the local bands of patriots which harassed the Italian positions that were also attacked by the RAF. Eventually, on 6 July, the Italian commander of Debra Tabor, having no prospect of relief, surrendered along with his more than 5,000 troops, among whom the colonial forces joined the British and became a patriot banda. Major Douglas, who had replaced Simonds, then focused on Kulkaber in order to cut the supply route from east of Lake Tana to Gondar. Poor weather and a shortage of supplies and money prevented Douglas from achieving any real success, the main operation against Gondar having to be delayed until the end of the rainy period in November. In the meantime, in view of the reorganization imposed by the British needs in North Africa, the Balkans and the Middle East, East Africa Force was replaced by East Africa Command, under direct orders from the War Office in London, on 15 September. The command, led by General Platt, covered the entire area from Eritrea to the Zambesi River and was divided into four areas, which included Ethiopia and British Somaliland under the 12th African Division and Central Command spreading from Kenya under the 11th

Italian General Ruggero Santini was hunted for three months before he gave himself up, surrendering to British forces. (Photo by Popperfoto via Getty Images)

African Division. Other than carrying out purely administrative duties, these commands were concerned with weapons control and the task of eliminating the last pocket of Italian resistance in the area. This task was planned from early September, in view of the end of the rainy season, with East Africa Command taking over responsibility for all activities in the region and putting 12th African Division in charge of all operations. This led to the initial plan to relieve the Sudan Defence Forces troops in the Wolchefit area with 25th and 26th East African Brigades, soon leading to the first step in the final operations of the East African campaign: the sudden surrender of the Wolchefit defenders on 27 September. This, resulting in the capture of some 3,000 Italian and colonial troops, was due to a combination of factors, ranging from shortage of food to large-scale desertions amongst colonial troops, RAF activity and the persistent threat posed by Arbegnoch forces.

The initial reaction was limited, both because of the need to repair the road and because it was acknowledged there was very little a single brigade could achieve. The main effort was to come from Debra Tabor, while troops approached Gondar from Wolchefit, making contact with the local patriots but taking no risks. The unusually long rainy season, lasting well into October, delayed the construction of the Debra Tabor road, leading to the decision to switch to the northern front in the belief that Nasi would be prone to surrender if attacked by a sizeable force. Orders

A caterpillar truck in action in the Lake Tana area of Ethiopia. British forces (African, Indian and South African) were compelled to do a great deal of work to improve communications in various areas of Ethiopia. (British Army, public domain, via Wikimedia Commons)

were issued on 27 October, with 25th East African Brigade to attack from the north on or about 9 November, while 26th East African Brigade was to pass through, clearing up Italian positions. Two days before the start of the operation, Lieutenant-Colonel Colling, commander of 1/6th King's African Rifles, was to move from the south, seizing Kulkaber and advancing to Gondar, while 2nd Ethiopian Battalion, along with the patriots, was to advance west of Lake Tana. A third column, comprising the Sudan Defence Force's Composite Battalion and other Arbegnoch forces, was to move on to Chilga. The RAF started bombing the Italian positions at once. After a failed attempt against the Gondar positions on 11 November, General Fowkes decided to add another column on 14 November, 25th East African Brigade moving from Dancaz to attack Kulkaber from the north. Simultaneously, an assault was to be mounted by the force from the south, which imposed a delay to the 21st. In the meantime, RAF attacks continued relentlessly and unhindered, with the last Italian aircraft flying on 20 November.

The final drive started on 20 November, 2nd Ethiopian Battalion advancing to the south of Gondar along a series of tracks south-west of Lake Tana, while the Sudan Column eventually attacked and clashed with the Italian defences at Chilga, but without success. The main assault focused on Kulkaber, defended by two Blackshirts battalions and one colonial battalion. On 21 November, 25th East African Brigade attacked Kulkaber, facing determined Italian resistance, which was soon overcome thanks to multiple assaults from different directions. Kulkaber surrendered during the afternoon, with the loss of some 2,400 prisoners. This paved the way for the attack against Gondar, which was to follow a similar pattern. The 26th East African Brigade was to strike from the east and 25th Brigade from the south, the bulk of the patriot fighters moving in the area between the two. From the north, the Argyll and Sutherland Highlanders were to contain as many enemy forces as possible in the Wolchefit area. To provide support, the RAF started striking Italian defences before preparations were completed, 26th Brigade struggling with unsuitable terrain and relying on mules to bring in supplies. The final attack started at 0530hrs on 27 November, with 26th Brigade advancing against Italian positions east of Gondar, the first objective being seized by 1400hrs. As the attack expanded, the Italians started withdrawing, only to fall into the arms of the patriot forces to the north and south. In the south, the Italian positions had been attacked the night before, some of them being seized by surprise, with the result that by 0800hrs on the 27th all the Italian defenders had been killed, enabling 26th Brigade to advance along the hills to the east of Azozo and eventually attack the place itself, which was seized at 1445hrs. 25th East African Brigade then continued to advance, facing only moderate opposition and reaching all its objectives by noon. Eventually, at 1540hrs, an Italian delegation arrived at Brigade Headquarters to ask for surrender. General Nasi was contacted and eventually surrendered the entire Italian garrison at Gondar. The last battle – although minor skirmishing continued in the months that followed against isolated pockets of Italian resistance – cost the British forces 32 killed, 182 wounded and six missing. Some 10,000 Italian and 12,000 colonial troops surrendered, their casualties being estimated at 4,000 killed and 8,400 sick or wounded.

ANALYSIS

British losses between June 1940 and May 1941 amounted to 1,154 battle casualties and 74,550 sick and injured, including some 20,000 cases of dysentery and malaria. By the end of the campaign, only some 80,000 Italian forces – colonial troops included – were left out of the 300,000 or so available in June 1940. The East African campaign cost the RAF 138 aircraft, a figure to which two Free French aircraft should be added. The Italians lost 250 out of the 325 aircraft available in the region. These figures alone show what can undoubtedly be considered an outstanding success, and indeed Britain's first victory against Axis forces during World War II. Some considerations are due, however. The victory achieved was not an easy one and the entire campaign was affected by other aspects of British strategy in the overall war.

In June 1940, Italian East Africa posed a significant threat to British positions in North Africa and the Red Sea, with a potential influence on the Arabian Peninsula and Indian Ocean. As such, the Italian threat could not be ignored, especially in view of the notable difference in size between the forces available to both sides. Even though the Italians did not pose a significant threat against Sudan or Kenya, their seizure of British Somaliland increased the potential threat against the Red Sea and Arabian Peninsula. In the autumn of 1940, it was already clear, however, that the Italian threat was not as significant as might have been expected, and the British could

Men from the Belgian Force Publique on their march to Ethiopia. As well as African, Indian and South African troops, soldiers from De Gaulle's Free French and from Belgium took part in the East African campaign. (Public domain via Wikimedia Commons)

therefore choose between two possible solutions: besieging Italian East Africa or removing the threat with a direct attack. The first option might have been preferable in view of the overall strategic situation (the planned attack in North Africa and the Italian–Greek war), but Wavell's decision to attack turned out to be the ideal solution. Relying on better-prepared and equipped, albeit inferior, forces, the main Italian positions were eliminated with a campaign lasting from December 1940 (when preparations started) to May 1941 (when Amba Alagi surrendered). This success was achieved in spite of the great disparity in forces, the difficult terrain and weather and the vast distances involved. The critical issue is whether some of the forces involved in the East African campaign, notably 4th Indian Division, might have provided decisive weight to alter the situation in North Africa, where another, more important success (strategically speaking) might have been achieved.

There is no possible answer to such a counterfactual question, but one can remark on Wavell's choice and the importance of the East African campaign. By eliminating a potential threat with a swift campaign, he was then able to focus on the other theatres of operations free from any concern. But did the strategic decisions made between the autumn of 1940 and spring of 1941, including the decision to attack in East Africa, influence other decision in North Africa and the Balkans? The answer is that they most certainly did, perhaps not because of the campaign itself but due to the scarcity of forces thus available to Wavell and the multiplicity of tasks he had to deal with.

Men from the Italian Africa Police (Polizia Africa Italiana, PAI). Other than regular army and colonial units, Italian police forces (Carabinieri, or military police) and the PAI took part in the fighting in East Africa. (LupusFido, CC BY-SA 3.0 https://creativecommons. org/licenses/by-sa/3.0, via Wikimedia Commons)

Seen from this angle, the campaign is even more important, as its excellent conduct enabled the eradication of a threat with the use of limited forces within a limited period of time. The commanders and the troops – Indian, South African and African – fought to such a level of excellence that one may consider this one of the most successful campaigns of the entire war. To what extent this was owed to the poor Italian fighting performance is another matter. There is no doubt that the Italians fought well, as they did at Keren and other places such as Gondar, their sudden collapse not due to their poor combat capabilities but to an almost complete lack of any strategic view. This was only partly down to Mussolini and the high command in Rome, who could only partly influence the decisions made on the spot by Amedeo d'Aosta, the regional commander. His lack of any

Men from the King's African Rifles collect surrendered Italian weapons at the Wolchefit Pass on 27 September 1941. This position, protecting the last Italian redoubt at Gondar, practically surrendered without a fight. (Lt H. J. Clements, No.1 Army Film and Photographic Unit, UK, Public domain, via Wikimedia Commons)

strategic view and inability to understand the limitations of his own forces and the capabilities of his opponents led to a campaign that was fought in a quite amateurish way: the entire frontier of Italian East Africa was defended, and any withdrawal was supposed to be to a series of strongholds that were simply expected to hold out indefinitely. Not surprisingly, the battle of Keren marked the peak of the campaign as it proved decisive in the defeat of the bulk of the Italian forces, which were in a hopeless position anyway following the successful crossing of the Juba River. By April 1941, the Italian defences were already doomed to failure, their withdrawal into the interior areas of Ethiopia merely enabling Cunningham and Platt to eliminate the pockets of resistance one by one.

Wavell's strategic grasp, albeit open to criticism, was undoubtedly much better than that of his opponent, who ended up making decisions to the advantage of his enemy. By the time Addis Ababa and Amba Alagi surrendered, Italy had ceased to be a real player in the war. This was mostly because of the defeats suffered in North Africa and against Greece, but was also due to the setbacks in East Africa, where the Italians had shown none of the imagination displayed by the British. The British commanders had managed to turn all the Italian advantages into disadvantages, which makes this campaign of particular interest. The East African campaign can thus be considered one of the key campaigns of World War II.

The Italians made extensive use of field-modified trucks or, as in this case, caterpillar trucks protected by metal plates or even wood. This vehicle is named Culqualber, Italian for Kulkaber. (Public domain via Wikimedia Commons)

THE BATTLEFIELD TODAY

There are not many battlefield tours in East Africa. The only one currently available relates to World War I. The campaign itself is largely overlooked in Britain, being relegated to examination by a relatively small group of enthusiasts in Italy. The area has been characterized by long-lasting wars. Eritrea, part of Ethiopia since 1952, fought a 30-year war for independence, while Ethiopia itself faced unrest and a kind of dictatorship from 1974. A coup took place in that year, installing what has been defined as a socialist government, but in reality the country was ruled by the military, which faced domestic resistance. The end of this period in 1991 did not mark the end of the country's troubles, however. The new government had to deal with protests, a continuation of the conflict with Eritrea and new problems with neighbouring Somalia, where Islamic terrorism was starting to grow. Somalia, which was under a United Nations-controlled Italian trusteeship after the war, has also had its own troubles. After the two parts of Somalia united and received independence in 1960, the country faced war, rebellion and, eventually, a devastating civil war, which lasted many years and paved the way for the establishment of terrorist groups in the country.

The political instability of the region surely discourages any potential battlefield tourists from visiting the area, which can nevertheless be extremely welcoming and has many sites of interest. Apart from the obvious growth of the urban areas, many of the World War II battlefields mentioned in this book have preserved their characteristics, better than many European ones, and can be explored. A stay will also enable the battlefield enthusiast to experience first-hand the climate – which will help them understand the conditions the soldiers endured during the campaign, especially those who were unaccustomed to the weather. Travelling across the country will also highlight the struggles the troops had in crossing very long distances on poor or non-existent roads. The East African battlefields are admittedly not the easiest to get to, but if you are adequately prepared and willing to undertake the task, they can be extremely interesting and satisfying.

FURTHER READING

Abyssinian Campaign (The). The Official History of the Conquest of Italian East Africa, HMSO, London (1942)

Air Historical Branch, 'The East African Campaigns 1940–1941', Royal Air Force Narrative, n.p. (n.d.)

Brett-James, Antony, *Ball of Fire. The Fifth Indian Division in World War II*, Gale & Polden, Aldershot (1951)

Crociani, Piero, *La Polizia dell'Africa Italiana (1937–1945)*, Ufficio Storico della Polizia di Stato, Rome (2009)

Del Boca, Angelo, *Gli italiani in Africa orientale*, Vol. III, *La caduta dell'Impero*, Laterza, Rome/Bari (1986)

Del Boca, Angelo, *The Ethiopian War*, The University of Chicago Press, Chicago/London (1969)

Diamond, Jon, *Orde Wingate*, Osprey, Oxford (2012)

Maravigna, Pietro, *Come abbiamo perduto la guerra in Africa*, Tosi, Rome (1949)

Marino, Francesco, 'Military Operations in the Italian East Africa, 1935–1941: Conquest and Defeat', MA Thesis, USMC Command and Staff College (2009)

Mockler, Anthony, *Haile Selassie's War. The Italian–Ethiopian Campaign, 1935–1941*, Random House, New York (1984)

Orpen, Neill, *East African and Abyssinian Campaigns*, South African Forces World War II, Vol. I, Purnell, Cape Town (1968)

Pearce, Jeff, *Prevail. The Inspiring Story of Ethiopia's Victory Over Mussolini's Invasion*, Skyhorse, New York (2014)

Platt, William, 'Operations of East Africa Command, 12 July, 1941 to 8 January 1943' in *Supplement to the London Gazette*, 16 July 1946, HMSO, London (1946)

Playfair, I. S. O. & Butler, J. R. M., *The Mediterranean and the Middle East*, History of World War II, United Kingdom Military Series, Vol. I, 'The Early Successes Against Italy (to May 1941)', Vol. II, 'The Germans Come to the Help of their Ally (1941)', HMSO, London (1954, 1956)

Prasad, Bisheshwar (ed), *East African Campaign, 1940–41*, The Official History of the Indian Armed Forces in World War II (1939–1945), Combined Inter-Services Historical Section (India & Pakistan), New Delhi (1963)

Raugh, H. E., *Wavell in the Middle East, 1939–1941. A Study in Generalship*, Brassey, London (1993)

Rovighi, Alberto, *Le operazioni in Africa Orientale (giugno 1940 – novembre 1941)*, Ufficio Storico Stato Maggiore Esercito, Rome (1995)

Rucker Snead III, Lawrence, 'Wavell's Campaigns in the Middle East: An Analysis of Operational Art and the Implications for Today', monograph, School of Advanced Military Studies, US Army Command and General Staff College, Fort Leavenworth (1994)

Scarselli, Aldo Giuseppe, 'Truppe Coloniali di Italia e Regno Unito in Africa Orientale: una comparazione (1924–1939), Ph.D. thesis, Florence University, Italy (2018)

Sobski, Marek, *East Africa 1940–1941 (land campaign): The Italian Army Defends The Empire in the Horn of Africa*, Zielona Gora, trans. Tomasz Basarabowicz (2020)

Stewart, Andrew, *The First Victory. The Second World War and the East African Campaign*, Yale University Press, New Haven/London (2016)

Sutherland, Jon & Canwell, Diane, *Air War in East Africa 1940–41. The RAF versus the Italian Air Force*, Pen & Sword, Barnsley (2009)

Ufficio Storico Stato Maggiore Esercito, Ministero della Difesa, *La guerra in Africa Orientale*, Ufficio Storico Stato Maggiore Esercito, Rome (1971)

Wavell, Archibald, 'Operations in East Africa, November, 1940 – July, 1941' in *Supplement to the London Gazette*, 10 July 1946, HMSO, London (1946)

Weller, George, *The Belgian Campaign in Ethiopia*, Belgian Information Center, New York (1941)

INDEX

Figures in **bold** refer to illustrations.